Nov, 2007

Be a good Coach

Love

Aunt Pat

UNDERTAKER'S SON

I have great respect for Digger Phelps, and it is not just that he was a major influence in the world of athletics—the leading basketball coach in the entire United States, in my opinion. My respect stems from the fact that Digger devotes a lot of time to helping other people.

When I was President, Digger's Weed and Seed Program was enormously effective in getting inner-city kids to stay away from drugs. He has done a lot more than that, too.

I am absolutely convinced that he is a true "Point of Light" who believes that service to others is a very important part of life.

—George H. W. Bush

UNDERTAKER'S SON

LIFE LESSONS FROM A COACH

Richard "Digger" Phelps

WITH JACK COLWELL

THE LYONS PRESS
Guilford, Connecticut
An imprint of The Globe Pequot Press

The Lyons Press is an imprint of The Globe Pequot Press.

10 9 8 7 6 5 4 3 2 1

Printed in the United States of America

Library of Congress Cataloging-in-Publication Data

Phelps, Richard.
Undertaker's son : life lessons from a coach / Richard "Digger" Phelps with Jack Colwell.
p. cm.
ISBN-13: 978-1-59921-209-8 (alk. paper)
1. Phelps, Richard. 2.Basketball coaches–United States–Biography. 3. Coaching (Athletics)–Philosophy. 4. Conduct of life. 5. Success. I. Colwell, Jack. II. Title.
GV884.P45A35 2007
796.323092–dc22
2007017197

CONTENTS

The Coach's Game Plan for Life viii

Stranger in Our House 1

Dad's Undertaking 5

Wizard Kicks ND: We Kick His Ass 13

"Jesus, Mary, and Joseph!": That's My Mom 21

You Can Go Home Again 29

Hail, Caesar 35

The Judge Ruled 45

My Most Important Game 51

Dreaming of Notre Dame 57

A Dream Comes True 67

Upsetting Experiences 75

Recruiting Promises 83

Always Have a Backup 89

Weeding and Seeding 97

Washington Sightseeing: Where Tourists Fear to Tread . . 105

Dan Quayle's Hot Potato(e) 113

Racing with Murphy Brown. 121

Foreign Policy: Is the President Naked Underneath? . 131

Voting in the Killing Fields. 139

A Russian I Couldn't Kill 149

Bob Knight and Al McGuire: On Court and Off 155

Digger as Artist and Van Gogh Freak. 165

One for the Gipper 171

Relax: Stress Is Stressful 179

Hesburgh Asks: "What Have You Really Been Doing?" . 187

Giving Volume to Small Voices. 195

High Schools: Warehousing, Not Educating. 203

The 2-Foot Yardstick 211

Shut Up and Sit Down on the Bench 221

The "Real" Dickie V 227

Digger for President: What If He Ran?. 233

Four Good Friends, Soon to Be Three 241

No Decade to Waste: Do It Yesterday 253

About the Authors 259

For my Mom and Dad,
who taught me how to live life

THE COACH'S GAME PLAN FOR LIFE

DO IT YESTERDAY. Tomorrow might not come. Knowing advice from an undertaker's son.

YOU CAN GO HOME AGAIN. A hometown can be a Beacon. Visit that old neighborhood.

HAVE A DREAM AND PURSUE IT. Lack of a dream for success can mean a nightmare of failure.

SHOOT FOR YOUR ULTIMATE GOAL. You just might make it. If you don't try, you can't get there.

ALWAYS HAVE A BACKUP. The best game plans don't prevent setbacks. Have alternatives.

GOD DIDN'T GIVE US THIS TIME TO WASTE. Have a purpose. Something more than wealth.

BE COLOR-BLIND. Racism is wrong morally and an obstacle economically in global competition.

MUSIC IS LIKE PIZZA. Pick musical toppings to suit your taste and mellow out to beat stress.

SAY THANKS TO THOSE WHO HELPED ALONG THE WAY. Give help unto others as others helped you.

SEEK SPIRITUAL FULFILLMENT. Find a site meaning to you what Notre Dame's Grotto means to me.

BE PUSHY WHEN IT COMES TO DEMANDING BETTER EDUCATION FOR THE KIDS. For the nation's future.

NEVER RETIRE. Maybe from a job. But not from life. Restart. Give back. Help out. Stay vital.

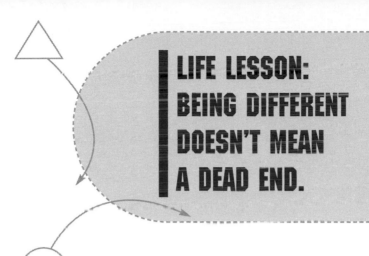

Chapter 1

Stranger in Our House

"Turned out that David, whose father worked at the Nabisco box factory down by the river, and Douglas, whose father was a driver for the guy who ran Matteawan State Hospital for the criminally insane, never had anyone sleeping in a box in their living rooms. Never. They never heard of such a thing. That's when I knew we were a little different."

One

One of my first vivid memories of childhood is of a morning when I was probably four years old, maybe five. I awoke at our home at 13 Cottage Place in the small city of Beacon, New York. That's where I was born on the Fourth of July in 1941. Beacon is on the Hudson River, about sixty miles north of New York City. To me, it's one of the greatest cities in the world. New York City? Sure. But I'm referring here to Beacon, the city to which I owe so much.

Well, I was ready that morning for a breakfast of Cheerios and fruit and then going out to play. How do I know it was Cheerios? Had to be. I insisted on it because Cheerios sponsored the *Lone Ranger* on the radio. Back at that age, I could recite the opening for the Lone Ranger, and I still can: "A fiery horse with the speed of light, a cloud of dust, and a hearty 'hi-yo Silver!'"

Later in play I might be the Lone Ranger as I joined David Ferris, who lived across the street, and Douglas Patterson, who lived next door, my two best neighborhood friends. We could play cowboys and Indians then, with no adult looking askance at what now might be deemed politically incorrect behavior. Funny, though, even if that was somehow incorrect, we lived in a city where we as children never were concerned whether folks in that melting pot were black or white; Irish or Dutch; Italian or German; Catholic, Protestant or Jewish; rich or poor.

That's one of the reasons I owe so much to Beacon. The lessons of the neighborhood from back then have helped me all my life in whatever I've accomplished. In coaching basketball at the University of Notre Dame, I was right at home in homes of outstanding black athletes we successfully recruited. Back in Beacon I sometimes was the only white kid playing hoops at a playground in a predominately black neighborhood. Never thought a thing about it. Nor did the kids with whom I played.

Heck, Beacon High School had a black quarterback, a hero for the younger kids, way back when I was in grade school. So it was amazing to me to hear of the ridiculous controversy decades later over whether blacks could play quarterback in college and the pros.

Then, when I moved from coaching college basketball to coaching the streets as a White House assistant to President George H. W. Bush, heading Operation Weed and Seed, I was able to go into some of the "worst" neighborhoods where others feared to enter. I understood the people and the problems. More importantly, people there understood that I understood. Lessons from Beacon helped me as we worked to weed out drugs, gangs, and violence and then seed the troubled area with programs to provide hope, jobs, and safety.

If only kids in those troubled neighborhoods had the opportunities I had in Beacon. My goal now is to help kids to have a better chance, with mentorships, with after-school programs in the hours when they get into trouble, with a return of neighborhood schools.

On that morning back at our home, I had no thoughts of the future, other than Cheerios and play. I climbed out of bed and, still in my pajamas, walked down the hallway that led from my room in the back corner of the house, past my parents' bedroom and by my little sister's room and down the stairs that led right into our living room.

Halfway down the staircase, I saw him. And I just stopped.

There was a guy sleeping in our living room. Sleeping in a box. He was all dressed up in a suit and tie. If he was sleeping, why wasn't he wearing his pajamas? And I remember thinking, "Whoa! What's that about?"

I sat down on the stairs. Sure didn't want to get in trouble for waking him up. Yet, I wanted to get my breakfast out of the way and go out to play. After a minute or two, I got up and walked down to the bottom of the stairs, careful not to make a sound, and slipped quietly through the living room and to the kitchen for breakfast. Success. I didn't wake up this guy sleeping in the box.

My dad was already at work, at a job I later was to understand. My mom was in the kitchen, ready with my cereal. As I spooned down the cereal with milk and probably a sliced banana, I asked my mother why the guy was sleeping in the living room.

"He's not sleeping, Richard," she told me. "That man died."

There was another person "in a box" at the funeral home, the one adjacent to our backyard, where my father earned a living as an undertaker. So, my mother explained, we needed to find another place to hold a wake for this other guy. That place was our living room.

This was the awakening for me. I was an undertaker's son. Later, in part because of that but also for a reason of which I'm not exactly proud, I was nicknamed "Digger."

When I finished my breakfast, I walked back through the living room, past the guy in the box, and went back upstairs to dress, not tiptoeing now. I didn't have to be quiet. No danger of awakening our guest. When I came back down, I didn't give him a second look, a second thought, and went out to play.

On the corner in front of our house, I met up with David and Douglas. Before we played cowboys and Indians or maybe it was a fistball game out in the street, I asked them some questions about their houses. Turned out that David, whose father worked at the Nabisco box factory down by the river, and Douglas, whose father was a driver for the guy who ran Matteawan State Hospital for the criminally insane, never had anyone sleeping in a box in their living rooms. Never. They never heard of such a thing.

That's when I knew we were a little different.

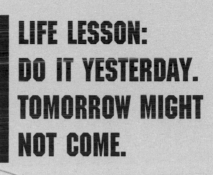

Chapter 2

Dad's Undertaking

"With perfect timing, he knew when to close the casket. That last moment was so important, and he sensed just when to tell the family to pay their last respects. 'I think it's time to get to the church,' he would say, kindly, knowing that tears would flow as the casket was closed. That was heavy. Somebody had to do it. My dad. That was his business, his job."

Two

Different we were but not in a negative way. Sure, we often focused on death, sometimes cutting summer vacation short because we had a customer. That was my father's business.

Growing up as an undertaker's son also gave me an appreciation of life and a determination to live every day to the fullest, not put off what you would like to do or should do. Death can come at any time even for the young. We read frequently about teenagers killed in auto accidents. Death can come when least expected. We know of friends or relatives or neighbors who suddenly, without warning, suffered a fatal heart attack.

Do it yesterday. Tomorrow might not come.

There were practical applications in being an undertaker's son. In college, I'd send flowers to girls all the time. They never knew how I could afford such beautiful bouquets until I invited them to visit home.

My father, also Richard Phelps, was known in the community as Dick, never as Digger. He grew up in an orphanage. He knew little about his parents or exactly when or why he was placed in the Methodist Home for Children in Williamsville, New York. He found that he was born on February 6, 1912, in Columbus, Ohio, and was placed in the orphanage, according to records of the home, through application by his father on January 1, 1918, when he was only five years old. His father, who apparently had suffered health problems, died fairly young. His mother went off to New York City to work as a governess. Dad had a sister who also was put up for adoption.

For many years, Dad didn't even know the whereabouts of his parents and sister. He grew up in the orphanage, finally to be brought out by an uncle, Dr. Charles Chamberlayne Phelps, the medical doctor in the small town of Sackets Harbor, New York. When Dad left the orphanage, he was fourteen.

Remarkably, he never expressed bitterness about the sad situation of childhood. His inspirational example encourages me today in my efforts to promote mentoring programs and after-school activities aimed at convincing kids, so many of them in single-parent homes, that they can be successful. If my dad, with no parent at all in his life as he grew up, could be a success, going from the orphanage to being salutatorian of his graduating class at Sackets Harbor High School and then to becoming a successful businessman and a damn good father, they can make it, too.

Eventually, my dad was able to find his mother and sister and meet with them. His father by then had died. How sad, never really to know your father. I knew and loved my father and was ready and willing to follow in his footsteps as an undertaker, with all its lessons of life and death, until basketball changed my career plans.

During his high school years, Dad showed his determination by becoming a varsity football regular at tackle, even though he weighed less than 150 pounds. After high school, he was in the Civilian Conservation Corps, a federal program to combat unemployment during the Depression. Seeking a trade, he went to Simmons School of Embalming in Syracuse, the school I once planned to attend. My dad even purchased property on which to build an additional funeral home after I joined the business. Game plans for basketball, however, were to replace planning for funerals.

It was 1938 when Dad came to Beacon to work for Fred Hignell, the undertaker who ran the funeral home Dad was later to buy and run after Mr. Hignell's death. When he came to Beacon, Dad lived in a rooming house near the house at 13 Cottage Place where my mother was born and lived and that was to become our family home. They met, fell in love, were married, and became a team in running the funeral business and raising my two younger sisters and me. (Thanks to a great honor from the city of Beacon, Cottage Place now is called Digger Phelps Court.)

My dad was an Episcopalian who regularly attended services and taught Sunday school at St. Luke's Episcopal Church. My mother, a Catholic, saw to it that my sisters and I were raised in the Catholic faith. There was sort of a compromise. We were raised Catholic, but Dad, a firm believer in public schools, didn't want us going to Catholic schools. Actually, my mother was an advocate of public schools as well, so that's where we went, with release time for Catholic instructions.

My father was a perfectionist. And he had a temper. Both are traits I inherited. At the funeral home, he was always in a suit and tie, always neat, always organized. He was precise in his planning and demanded neatness, punctuality, and attention to detail from the off-duty policemen and firemen he hired as pallbearers and drivers.

In embalming, too, he was a perfectionist. It used to amaze me when I'd hear people coming out of the funeral home saying of the deceased things like, "He looks ten years younger." And I'd think, "He's dead. What are you talking about?" But my dad had a reputation as a great embalmer. I remember thinking when President Eisenhower died that they should have sent Dad to Washington for the embalming. Wasn't he the best in the country?

Everybody was treated the same, all with respect, at Dad's funeral home, whether the deceased was rich or poor, black or white, Catholic, Protestant, or Jew. This is one reason why at Dad's own funeral, there were members of the clergy of all three faiths officiating.

If a family could afford only a cheap casket that Dad didn't think would look right, he'd upgrade it without additional charge. But he had to pay the full bill from the casket company, resulting in struggles at times to make ends meet. Still, he would think of people first, money second, taking care of those who had lost a loved one, with a sense of touch and timing.

Every flower selection arriving for a funeral was marked down and described on a card, and Dad insisted on accuracy in the listings so the family knew exactly what was sent by whom. At an early age I helped with the cards and learned every type of flower.

I'd watch him helping the family of the deceased. Helping to pick out a suit or a dress. Helping to choose the casket. Helping to deal with the grief. He'd just take over for a family that had lost a loved one. For three days, they trusted my mom and dad to get them through the crisis, this event of sorrow.

With perfect timing, he knew when to close the casket. That last moment was so important, and he sensed just when to tell the family to pay their last respects. "I think it's time to get to the church," he would say, kindly, knowing that tears would flow as the casket was closed. That was heavy. Somebody had to do it. My dad. That was his business, his job.

His sensitivity toward the family was something I remembered in recruiting college basketball players. Families of those kids were concerned as well, not about a final journey, but in what I was telling them about getting a young man ready for a life journey. I learned a lot from Dad—talking to families, organizing, discipline, structure, and demanding perfection.

An undertaker has to develop a certain immunity about death. You distance yourself, build a wall. It's a protective mechanism so that you remain a pillar of strength for the grieving family and don't let yourself become too emotional. I wondered how my dad did it. The first time he cried, he told me, was when my Uncle Jimmy's wife, Aunt Katherine, died. That was the first time he had to embalm and bury a member of his own family.

Dad became a civic leader in Beacon. I remember when he was president of the Kiwanis Club and arranged a big pancake-day event. Aunt Jemima, she of pancake fame, arrived by helicopter for this big day for a little town, with a parade and all. Lots of pancakes were sold, and it proved to be one heck of a fund-raiser for community projects.

When I was in Little League baseball, Dad took an interest in the program and was instrumental in the building of a new field that's still in use today. So is the pool at the country club, with a wading pond next to it. Dad was responsible for that as well.

Another event Dad headed was the Soap Box Derby. My sister Diane wanted to enter, but no girl ever had. My dad, ahead of the time, said there was no reason why she couldn't race. Also, however, he told Diane that she couldn't accept the top prize if she won. The reason? Since he was running the event, it would give an appearance of a conflict of interest for one of his kids to get the prize. She raced, didn't win but set a precedent that girls could enter the event.

Now the temper.

One hot summer day when I was twelve or thirteen and feeling my oats, I came over from the house to help with a funeral. All the cops and firemen hired by Dad were, as he always insisted, dressed in suits and ties. Not me. No jacket. The guys got on me: "Where's your jacket?"

"Too hot," I told them. They laughed, knowing what was coming.

When Dad arrived, he glared at this son who was not dressed to the desired perfection. "If you're not gonna dress right, then go home," he thundered. So I went home, changed clothes, got on my bike and rode over to the country club to go swimming. Just as I got to the club lot, a station wagon—our station wagon—pulled in, smoking. "Get your ass home and get to that funeral," was the short and stern admonition.

Home I went. Into a suit and tie I changed, and back to the funeral home I raced. The guys were really laughing at me now. "As soon as I take over this business, I'm firing all of you," I told them.

That was my dad. No fooling around. If I flunked a test or got in trouble at school, he'd smack me one. When I was a high school junior, I blew off a paper for English class, and the teacher called home. Dad called me by several names other than Richard, threw things, and swatted me. I thought I was going to die.

Now, let me be clear that I'm not talking about some kind of child abuse. Never did I suffer any injury other than to my pride. A swat in the proper place was a way to get my attention. Kind of like the nuns used to do with a ruler on the knuckles. He needed to get my attention.

Yep, he could yell. And so could I. Just as he'd holler at some funeral driver who didn't understand that he expected perfect timing in the departure of the procession to the cemetery, I'd yell at a player from whom I expected more effort: "You missed blocking out for the rebound again. We've been going over this since October. And it's January. That's three months! You still don't get it? Well, sit down on the bench! You're gonna stay there for the rest of the season!" (As you probably suspect, I would have added a couple of choice adjectives and perhaps an additional noun, verb, or gerund. But I don't intend this to be a book that seeks to shock with the strong lingo that coaches use to get the attention of some of their macho college athletes.)

When I coached, Dad was often able to attend games, especially if we were back East, say, in Madison Square Garden, the Meadowlands, or the Palestra in Philly. I'd invite him into the locker room. At halftime, I'd be screaming and yelling and cursing about what we'd done wrong. Sometimes, I'd look over and wink at him. After the game, I'd say, "That sounded familiar, didn't it?" Neither of us could take poor performance.

Sometimes when I thought he'd be furious, Dad would surprise me. Near the end of my senior year, when I threw a teacher's desk out the window and was accused of starting a riot at Beacon High School, I thought he was going to kill me, just beat me up and throw me in the morgue. Instead, he was good about it. He knew I wasn't trying to start a riot. So he concentrated on making sure I wasn't blamed unfairly for all that happened that wild day and that I would graduate. (More later about the dumped desk. I'm going to tell the truth about mistakes as well as successes.)

Since my dad was an Episcopalian, he didn't grow up rooting for the Catholics at Notre Dame. West Point is just down the Hudson from Beacon, so it was natural that he was for Army in those legendary football clashes with Notre Dame in the late 1940s. As kids back then, we'd play football with somebody pretending to be Johnny Lujack, famed quarterback of Notre Dame, and other kids being Doc Blanchard and Glenn Davis, the "Mr. Inside" and "Mr. Outside" of the great Army backfield.

When my dream came true and I became the coach at Notre Dame, Dad, of course, switched allegiance to the Irish. Luckily, with no scheduled funerals right then, he made it to South Bend in time for the game with UCLA on January 19, 1974, when my underdog Irish team broke the eighty-eight-game winning streak of the UCLA dynasty. It was the second most important coaching triumph of my career. Second most important? I'll explain that ranking later.

Was Dad a Notre Dame fan by then? You bet.

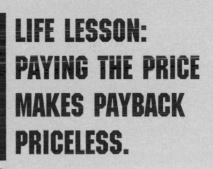

LIFE LESSON: PAYING THE PRICE MAKES PAYBACK PRICELESS.

Chapter 3

Wizard Kicks ND: We Kick His Ass

"One team did run up the score. John Wooden's UCLA. When we played his No. 1 team in Los Angeles, Wooden still had his starters in and was pressing with eight minutes left and a forty-one-point lead. UCLA did score over one hundred. It was 114–58. Late in the debacle, I caught the eye of an assistant UCLA coach and mouthed two words. They were not 'thank you.' And I suggested that he pass on my salutation to the Wizard of Westwood.

The message apparently was delivered. After the game, Wooden told me he wasn't running up the score, just getting his starters some needed work because final exams had kept them from practice. I knew the real reason. He was still miffed at Notre Dame for the Carr-led victory over UCLA in South Bend in 1971. So I told Wooden: 'John, you do anything you have to do to beat me because someday I'm going to kick your ass.'

This is one of the reasons that the kick we administered to end the UCLA streak was extra special."

Three

That 1974 victory over UCLA, regarded still as one of basketball's biggest upsets, was a dramatic come-from-behind win by a point over a coaching legend, John Wooden, acclaimed as "the Wizard of Westwood," and over a team with the top talent in the land. UCLA was led by Bill Walton, who now annoys many TV viewers with his distinctive voice and unusual analysis of basketball games. Back then, the big redhead was a superstar center for UCLA, intimidating on defense and in rebounding and about as unlikely to miss a shot as Cal Ripken was to miss a baseball game.

Ending the eighty-eight-game winning streak of a dynasty was of course a highlight of my coaching career—the second most important game ever for me. Without success in a game before I ever got to Notre Dame, as I'll explain, I never would have had a college head-coaching career.

Beating UCLA on that January 19 was special personally for me for reasons beyond the obvious one of breaking the record winning streak of the No. 1 team, with the No. 1 player and the No. 1 overall talent. Here's a little background.

First of all, although I had achieved my dream of being the head basketball coach at Notre Dame, the dream could have become a nightmare if my team continued to lose as often and as decisively as it had in my first season, 1971–72, as Irish coach. Our record was 6–20. This was a dream job? Was Notre Dame only a football school athletically, with neither players nor fans much interested in achievements with a ball that's round?

The great Austin Carr, who still holds Notre Dame scoring records, had graduated. He had led the Irish back in January of 1971 in inflicting the last defeat of UCLA prior to the start of their streak. Not much was left, and injuries took a toll on the returning players. I had to borrow three football players from Ara Parseghian and get a couple of baseball players to fill out the roster.

Our most pathetic performance was against Bob Knight's Indiana team in Bloomington, where they were dedicating Assembly Hall. We lost. Big. By a 94–29 score. Bob is my friend. Had been and still is. He did not try to run up the score. IU could have scored way over a hundred if Bob had wanted to pour it on. We were just terrible. After the game, a buddy from back in New York called to say the wire service transposed the numbers in our score. He thought it must have been 94–92. "Yeah," I told him. "We lost on a shot at the buzzer."

One team did run up the score. John Wooden's UCLA. When we played his No. 1 team in Los Angeles, Wooden still had his starters in and was pressing, with eight minutes left and a forty-one-point lead. UCLA did score over one hundred. It was 114–58. Late in the debacle, I caught the eye of an assistant UCLA coach and mouthed two words. They were not "thank you." And I suggested that he pass on my salutation to the Wizard of Westwood.

The message apparently was delivered. After the game, Wooden told me he wasn't running up the score, just getting his starters some needed work because final exams had kept them from practice. I knew the real reason. He was still miffed at Notre Dame for the Carr-led victory over UCLA in South Bend in 1971. So I told Wooden, "John, you do anything you have to do to beat me because someday I'm going to kick your ass."

This is one of the reasons that the kick we administered to end the UCLA streak was extra special. Lest any reader conclude that I didn't respect John Wooden, let me stress that the opposite is true. As a young coach, I studied and marveled at his devastating zone press. His amazing record—ten national championships, seven in a row—will never be matched. Talent is more widespread now. He had tremendous talent and knew how to utilize it to build dominant teams.

But a key to beating Wooden's team to end the streak was to avoid being intimidated. Many opponents were beat at the tip-off. They were in awe of the UCLA stars. They were terrified by the UCLA press. I stood up to Wooden not to show disrespect but to show I would not be intimidated and neither would my players.

We were improving in my second season, '72–'73. We returned to respectability with a winning record, 18–12, and received an invitation to play in the National Invitational Tournament. The NIT back then was a major tournament, not looked upon as it is today as the refuge of teams not good enough to make the NCAA field. Not only did we play in the NIT, we darn near won the tournament. Led by John Shumate, the best center I ever was privileged to coach, we won three tournament games, including victories over Southern Cal, Louisville, and North Carolina, all teams that would now have made it to the expanded NCAA tournament. Shu finally was back after missing my first season due to a life-threatening blood clot that endangered his heart. We lost in the championship game in New York City's Madison Square Garden to Virginia Tech by a point in overtime.

Improved though we were, we still weren't good enough to beat mighty UCLA. We lost in Los Angeles but only by twenty-six points this time. Then Wooden brought his No. 1 power to South Bend in January of 1973. Somehow, Notre Dame always seemed to be in the key game in the streak—last team to beat 'em before they started beating everybody as well as the team to beat 'em again to end that eighty-eight-game streak. Also, in that game in South Bend in 1973, UCLA was seeking to set the record at that time for consecutive wins. They were tied with the great San Francisco teams of the Bill Russell era in the mid-1950s at sixty straight wins.

They got the record, beating my team for the fourth straight time, in an 82–63 game in which we at least stood up to intimidation and began to shake up the intimidators. Shumate wouldn't back down in guarding Walton. Neither Walton nor Wooden, it seemed, was used to a rival center daring to play such tough defense against the UCLA star. *Sporting News* reported that Wooden "took a stroll down to the Notre Dame bench in the second half to tell Phelps that John Shumate had 'lost his composure' in a sudden tiff with Walton."

Well, what Wooden told me was, "Tell John Shumate to lay off the rough play on Walton or I'll put Sven Nater into the game to play rough." Nater, a tough, talented backup center, could come in with no concern about how much he fouled Shumate. Well, I didn't want any of my players injured. Nor did I want to see Walton or any of the UCLA players injured. But it was kind of like in baseball, where nobody wants a beanball war, but any team with any baseballs must make clear that it will retaliate if its batters are knocked down. So I told Wooden, "Go ahead and bring in Nater. I've got three football players at the end of my bench, and I'll put all three in the game and take on your entire team." The game went on without incident.

Wooden apologized in a letter after the season. *Sporting News* quoted Walton as saying Shumate apologized to him for any misunderstanding. But the publication also noted that Shumate "couldn't understand what all the excitement was about, saying that Walton not only had been giving him a working-over but calling him names, too."

To me, this was just another case of attempted intimidation, another reason we would not back down even if we lacked the firepower to win, another indication that we would win when we were on a more equal basis with UCLA. Also, it's another explanation of why that win, when it came, was so special.

We were really good in '73–'74, attracting national attention and moving up the poll rankings to No. 2, right behind mighty UCLA. We had all five starters back, plus the addition of Adrian Dantley, a freshman who was to go on to be one of the most prolific scorers in college and in the NBA. Dantley was amazing as he battled under the basket at only 6-foot-5, often half a foot shorter than the opponents he outrebounded, outhustled, outplayed, and outscored.

Still, could the "football school" really win a big basketball game, biggest of the season, against a basketball dynasty? Would Notre Dame students show up and show the passion they always displayed at a football game? Was I right about the prospect of basketball success at Notre Dame, or was I a dope for thinking I could produce a basketball winner where football was king? If Notre Dame could beat UCLA, we would be ranked No. 1, bringing about the rare ratings of the same college at the top in both football and basketball.

Football supremacy was no shock. Notre Dame was—and is again under Charlie Weis—a football power, a contender for a national championship. When I came to Notre Dame, Ara Parseghian was the football coach, a great coach to whom I had written a letter back in 1965, when I was a high school coach. I poured out my heart about my love for Notre Dame and my desire to coach there someday.

"Someday" was here. And Notre Dame was No. 1 in football. Just three weeks prior to the UCLA game, on New Year's Eve in the Sugar Bowl in New Orleans, Ara's team defeated Bear Bryant's Alabama, which had been ranked No. 1. The thrilling one-point victory catapulted Notre Dame to the national championship.

Two of the most exciting plays in the long history of Irish athletics occurred in that three-week period. In football, it was a pass to a seldom-used tight end named Robin Weber, a sophomore who had caught only one pass before in his collegiate career. Situation: Third and 8 for Notre Dame on its own 4-yard line as it clung to a precarious one-point lead, 24–23, in the final minutes of the game. Failure on third down would mean a punt to Alabama, which then would have good field position and two minutes to score, with only a field goal needed. What would Ara do?

Running play to keep the clock moving and hope at least to get a bit farther away from the end zone?

Passing play, with the risk of a fatal interception but the possibility of hitting All-American end Dave Casper for a first down?

Ara risked a pass. Casper was the intended receiver. But Ara stressed—as I was to stress with my team—to always have a backup. He trusted his quarterback, Tom Clements, to understand this and deliver under pressure.

Clements, back in his own end zone, saw that Casper was covered but Weber, racing down the field, was open. Ball in the air. It seemed to Notre Dame fans at the game and watching on TV, as they held their breath, that the ball was floating in the air forever. Weber caught the 36-yard pass. First down. Notre Dame, out of danger, would win and be No. 1.

Within three weeks, there came another time when Irish fans held their breath at our Athletic and Convocation Center or watching on TV as a ball, this one round, was in the air with just twenty-nine seconds left to play and UCLA ahead of us by a point.

UCLA had been ahead by a lot more than that. They took a 70-59 lead with just three minutes and thirty-two seconds left, a seemingly safe lead for the No. 1 Bruins back at the time when there was no shot clock and no three-point shot to help the trailing team.

I called time-out. Shumate, on the thirtieth anniversary of our historic win, was quoted in the Notre Dame student newspaper as recalling my determination: "I can still see the snarl, the passion in his eyes, the belief and his love for Notre Dame. He pointed to each and every one of us. He said, 'If you don't believe that we can do this, then leave and go to the locker room right now. If you stay here and believe, then we can do this.'" Also, I went to a three-guard look with Shumate moved to the top of the press.

UCLA never scored again. As we hit shots and our crowd roared as loud as ever at a football game, it could be that the intimidators were intimidated. We certainly were no longer awed by the UCLA mystique.

Dwight Clay took the dramatic shot that put us ahead. Unlike Weber, he was a regular, and he had earned the nickname of "the Iceman" by hitting a shot the year before that ended Marquette's eighty-one-game home winning streak. But he had hit only one basket so far on this day. And he wasn't the player who was supposed to shoot. It was Gary Brokaw, another guard, a guard who was hot. But Brokaw, when he got the ball, was closely defended, unable to get off a shot. Gary knew how to find a backup under pressure. Clay, like Weber in the football classic, was left open. Brokaw hit Clay with a pass in the right corner. Clay swished the shot. And we held on despite a flurry of UCLA attempts in those last twenty-nine seconds. We won. We, like the football team, were No. 1.

We had practiced long and hard for this upset. And not just practice for coping with individual UCLA players and the Wooden system. On the Wednesday before the big Saturday game, I had the players practice cutting down the nets. To build their confidence, I told them that they would be cutting down the nets in celebration when the game ended and they ought to know how to do it with style as fans around the nation watched on TV and photographers took their pictures.

To have my parents there to witness the big win and to enjoy the celebration after the game meant a lot to me. They both were proud. They deserved to be. If it were not for all that they did for me, with discipline, guidance, patience, support, and love, this undertaker's son from little Beacon never would have been in his dream job on this day of triumph.

Dad was excited, of course. Characteristically, however, he was more restrained than my mother. She was celebrating with the abandon and zeal of the students who poured onto the court. No surprise. What a fan! When we had beaten Southern Cal on St. Patrick's Day the season before in the NIT, there was Maggie, my mother, amidst the students on the floor, celebrating in her green dress, dancing with Dave Casper, that All-American tight end from the football team.

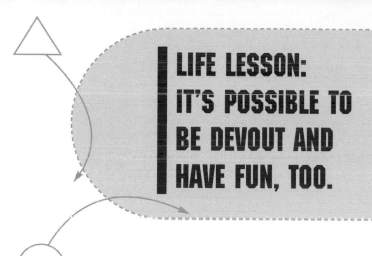

**LIFE LESSON:
IT'S POSSIBLE TO
BE DEVOUT AND
HAVE FUN, TOO.**

Chapter 4

"Jesus, Mary, and Joseph!": That's My Mom

"She was a typical Irish Catholic mom of that era, very religious, with an unshakable faith. For much of her life, she went to Mass and received Communion daily. She prayed the Rosary and had rosary beads all around the house, always handy for a few moments of prayer and meditation. Her faith, however, was not somber but joyous, not one of frowning at every little indiscretion but one of laughing and joking about any relatively inconsequential blunder or fault. She would cheat at bingo. Not for some tiny prize, but for the fun of it."

Four

Well, some people might be surprised, even shocked, to see their mother out on a basketball court, dancing with an All-American football player, amidst a wild victory celebration after a big win. Not me. Let me tell you about my mom, Maggie.

While my father came to Beacon as an adult, my mother was born there on April 18, 1918, in the house that became our family home. Mom was Irish. Really Irish, through ancestry and in her Irish Catholic outlook on life and death. Her great-grandparents were born in Ireland and came to this country in the mid-1800s. She had an Irish wit. She was the humorous one, the trickster in the family, always pulling jokes, making people laugh, brightening their spirits. She cared about people and had a big heart.

While I have my father's demand for perfection and temper, I got from Mom a sense of humor and my reputation as a prankster—some would say as a troublemaker—and my caring about people. The Irish have a way with words. I inherited that, even though I can't spell all of them.

Like most sons, I guess, I was closer to my mother. Once I was in college and was old enough to get away with it, I called her Maggie. The name fit her perfectly, and darn near everybody in Beacon knew Maggie. On Main Street in Beacon, a short walk between stores that should take two minutes would take her twenty minutes; she stopped to talk to everybody she knew, and that was half the town. With her involvement in so many activities, she really was the PR person for my father's business, getting people to know us, trust us, and remember us when somebody in their family died.

When I'd call home in later years, I'd say, "What's new, Maggie?" She'd often start out, "So-and-so's in the hospital, but they'll probably have Halvey." That was the rival funeral home. Indeed, the business always was as important to her as to Dad.

Often, in typical Irish Catholic fashion, she invoked the names of the Holy Family, exclaiming in a variety of circumstances, "Jesus, Mary, and Joseph!" Never was it swearing. "Jesus, Mary, and Joseph!" she would pray when hearing bad news about a family illness or fearing danger from an approaching storm. "Jesus, Mary, and Joseph!" she would laugh after her joke or a prank had everybody laughing—sort of a prayerful thanks for permitting such a good time.

"Jesus, Mary, and Joseph!" she would exclaim after I had done something wrong, calling, in effect, for divine help "to let me deal with this child and to let him cause less trouble." "Glory be to God" was her other favorite expression, spoken in response to any good news or surprising development, an expression of faith.

She was a typical Irish Catholic mom of that era, very religious, with an unshakable faith. For much of her life, she went to Mass and received Communion daily. She prayed the Rosary and had rosary beads all around the house, always handy for a few moments of prayer and meditation. Her faith, however, was not somber but joyous, not one of frowning at every little indiscretion but one of laughing and joking about any relatively inconsequential blunder or fault. She would cheat at bingo. Not for some tiny prize but for the fun of it. Like my mother, I have faith in God, a spiritual side, but not her devotion to unquestioning, formal practice of religion.

Maggie's great-grandfather was Francis Timoney, born August 4, 1829, in County Fermanagh, Ireland. At age twenty-three, he came to America, where he found work in a brickyard in New York. In three years, he became the foreman. Soon thereafter he purchased a half interest in the business. This remarkable story of success in America continued as he became sole owner of the yard and later bought three other brickyards at Duchess Junction. His yards turned out a quarter million bricks a day. He owned two barges on which the bricks were transported down the Hudson River to build New York City.

The Timoneys were wealthy beyond any dreams in the old country. They developed other businesses in an area near the yards that became known as Timoneyville.

Then, as the American dream became a nightmare for so many during the Great Depression, they lost virtually everything. My mother recalled going with her mother as a little girl on a horse-pulled wagon to take supplies and money for workers at the brickyard complex.

Other Irish ancestors in Beacon included my grandfather, James Sullivan, who ran a bar on Bank Street. Never drank, just poured. That's the way to be successful in the bar business.

Francis J. Sullivan, Maggie's brother, who had been a local high school basketball hero—left-handed, like me—died when he was only twenty years old. Believe it or not, he died from a blood blister that became infected. No penicillin was available then. It killed him. Today, it would not have been fatal or even serious.

For my mother, who was only eleven when her brother died, this was a shattering experience. Her parents were so aggrieved by the loss of a son shortly before Christmas that they could not celebrate the holiday ever again. No Christmas was celebrated at 13 Cottage Place until after my mother and father were married and moved to the old family home after I was born. Maybe the lack of Christmas for so long was why my mother made sure it was so special for us.

Every part of the house was decorated. A manger scene was a centerpiece. We would drive to one of those places where you could chop down your own Christmas tree. We always picked a beautiful tree, and then, maybe because the tree hanging out of our station wagon obstructed Dad's view, or maybe because other drivers were filled with too much Christmas cheer, we seemed every other year to have an accident on the way home. Nothing serious—we survived, and so did the Christmas trees. Once when

I was old enough to drive, I had an accident on the way back with the tree aboard, and I survived my father's anger.

When my sisters and I were little, my mom would wake us up early on Christmas morning when it was still dark. We would walk down the stairs from our rooms, but we couldn't get a glimpse of the living room, where we knew, or at least hoped, that our stockings would be filled with gifts and that bigger presents would be piled around the tree.

Off to Mass we would go. Church before presents. Mass was in Latin back then, and as I will explain later, Latin was not a language with which I ever developed an expertise. While I would pray in proper devotion, I would add a prayer, never answered, that the Christmas Mass would be short. Getting back home to see what was under the tree was my priority.

My sisters and I would run home, open the sliding doors to the living room and look at what was in the stockings we had hung on Christmas Eve. Mom would pass out the presents, some from Santa, some from our parents. She knew exactly for whom the presents were intended; she had wrapped them all, including the ones from Santa.

Santa knew what we wanted. I'd write letters to him on behalf of all the members of our family, including Bullets, our dog, and even our goldfish. Mom saved a copy of one of my letters. Unfortunately, it fell into the hands of my sister Diane, who threatened to make it public. Seems there were a few silly mistakes, such as the future Notre Dame basketball coach misspelling some words and writing "basket ball" as two words. Sisters do things like that, not necessarily for blackmail purposes but just for the glee of embarrassing a brother. Maybe it was Diane's way of getting back at me for my inappropriate nicknames for her. First it was "Joey," because I had wanted a baby brother when she was born. And I guess she was embarrassed when we both were in college and I'd spot her and holler, "Hey, Piggy!" It was a term of endearment, but maybe outsiders didn't always understand.

My plea to Santa, dated November 26, 1955, was the one that Diane threatened to have published. Well, here it is, published by me, even though Diane never really would do so herself. Kidding aside, we are very close.

My lengthy letter began: "We are writing too you too tell you what we would like too have for Christmas. We all tried too be helpful and be good around the house but, sometimes we were bad. So, we know you can't give us of the things we ask for because there are other children you have too give things too." OK, I got too carried away with an extra "o" in "to." But at least I was consistent.

And, yes, by fourteen, I knew our parents, not Santa, brought the presents. Diane, eleven then, also knew. But Barb, at seven, still believed, and that letter was really for her. I listed thirty-one gifts Barb wanted, everything from a pogo stick to a doll with hair, from a Howard Johnson dairy bar and soda fountain to a trumpet, from a nurse outfit to a lead pencil.

Diane wanted thirty presents, including a perfume kit, boy's dungarees, jewelry, a Dragnet Badge game, Nancy Drew books, the game Sorry! and "a lot in her stocking."

For me there was a modest request for twenty-two presents. Underlined as top priority was an electric football game. Also I requested that "basket ball" game, Hardy Boys books, a winter jacket for school, ice skates, model boats, and "anything else you have for me."

Bullets the dog wanted a steak. The fish wanted "stuff for the filter" to keep the water cleaner.

Santa was asked also to provide our parents with clothes they would want because they deserved a lot of presents. Well, they did, even if a reader might conclude, accurately I suppose, that praise for them was a bit self-serving in a request list for me that they would see.

The gifts they bought for us would be hidden up in the funeral-home showroom. On Christmas Eve, from my window on the second floor of our home, I could look out over the backyard and the path from the funeral home. I'd spy from there until I saw them bringing the presents, not yet wrapped. Some I could identify, some that I was pretty sure were for me. Some knowledge of what to expect always has been important to me, whether it was snooping around on Christmas Eve as a kid or scouting an opponent in basketball.

I remember my first kiss. Most people do. In high school perhaps? Or in junior high? My first kiss was in kindergarten. I kissed Nancy Farrell, a smooch as we stood on the sidewalk after leaving school. I thought she was cute, and I just kissed her on the cheek and ran home. Even then, my mother should have figured out that her hope of my becoming a priest wasn't going to materialize.

Mom would chaperone at CYO (Catholic Youth Organization) dances. Probably part of the willingness to volunteer was to make sure I wasn't kissing any more girls like I did in kindergarten.

Mom always got along with my wife, Terry. When our lives were to go in different directions and we were divorced, I kind of think Mom wondered if that was a mixed blessing, freeing me to consider belatedly the priesthood.

After my father died, Maggie lived for a time in her Beacon home. Neighborhoods change, for the worst at that time in Beacon. Though the nearby Main Street now flourishes again, it fell victim to that downtown downturn familiar then in many cities. She reluctantly moved to an assisted-living home, a place called New Horizons in Marlboro, Massachusetts. She was feisty as ever. They'd play games. She'd cheat at bingo, at blackjack, just for the fun, and still as always go to Mass.

Maggie died on December 30, 2003, at age eighty-five, granted extra years of her life to make life more enjoyable, more fun, for others.

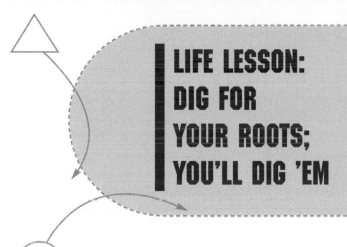

LIFE LESSON: DIG FOR YOUR ROOTS; YOU'LL DIG 'EM

Chapter 5

You Can Go Home Again

"On the streets of Beacon, I grew up, learning lessons that made me who I am and helped me to opportunities and whatever successes I've had—from Beacon to Notre Dame to the White House and beyond. Lessons on those streets were far different from what kids learn too many times on the streets of our cities today."

Five

Beacon, my hometown, was a great place for a kid to grow up in the 1940s and 1950s. This small city in New York on the east bank of the Hudson River is rich in history. It was incorporated in 1913 by combining the villages of Fishkill Landing and Matteawan. But its history can be traced back to the seventeenth century and settlement by the Dutch. The community is at the foot of Mount Beacon, atop which blazed historic beacon fires during the Revolutionary War, a means of signaling movement of British troops to alert the forces and supporters of General Washington. Still standing is the historic Madam Brett House, built in 1709. Washington was among the distinguished guests who stayed there.

The population of Beacon was about 12,500 in 1940 and grew to 14,000 in 1950. It was thriving then. Main Street was indeed the main street, a bustling commercial area of locally owned businesses just a couple of blocks from our house. It offered everything, from butcher to baker to candy maker, from groceries to hardware, from clothes and furniture to a service station with real service for motorists. As a kid about nine or ten, I'd wash windows of the cars of motorists who pulled in to get five bucks worth of gas at Cadmus Gulf Service. My pay was tips, maybe just a dime. But that was important. For a dime I could go down Main Street to Schuman's Army & Navy Store and buy a pink rubber ball for our fistball games. If tips were generous, I could also go to the Alps Sweet Shop for one of their wonderful hot fudge sundaes.

For adults, there were bars and banking and stores to buy just about anything folks in Beacon needed in those days—no need to drive to a shopping mall. And of course back then there were no shopping malls with the myriad franchises that unfortunately have replaced so many of the mom-and-pop stores where the customers were known by name and treated as neighbors, which in fact they were.

On the streets of Beacon, I grew up, learning lessons that made me who I am and helped me to opportunities and whatever successes I've had—from Beacon to Notre Dame to the White House and beyond. Lessons on those streets were far different from what kids learn too many times on the streets of our cities today.

The only drugs for sale I ever heard about were at J. Scott Nerrie's Pharmacy. No need for my parents to worry about what kind of movies their children would see if we went to the Beacon Theater. If kids got into a fight back then—and I don't want to suggest all of us boys were little angels—it involved mostly shoving, not shooting. Lessons on Beacon's streets were of people of various ethnic backgrounds and religions working together, getting along.

There were Jewish proprietors, at Schuman's, Gold's Meat Market, and Rosenblum's Shoes. My barber was Italian. There was a Dutch bakery. Nerrie's Pharmacy was run by an Englishman. There were Irish bars and Italian bars. While the Irish naturally tended to congregate in the Irish bars, Italians who stopped in were welcome, just as many an Irishman quenched his thirst in friendly fashion at an Italian bar.

The Alps and George's were run by Greek brothers, Pete and George Charkalis, who came to this country in 1920. I still love the chocolate at the Alps. On a visit home recently I got carried away and bought $117 worth of chocolate candy. Not all for me, just most of it. George's restaurant was our high school hangout, where we'd go after the Friday night games.

It just never occurred to me to look down on any ethnic group. No reason to. No prejudice against any ethnic group, religion, or race ever was expressed by my parents. Sure, unfortunately, housing was segregated. Blacks lived in one section of the city. For some reason, I never thought much about why that was. I'd go there as a kid to play basketball or other sports, neither fearing nor finding any racial hostility.

Streets were for play. Fistball was a favorite, played in the street in front of our home. Since we couldn't swing away at a baseball on a neighborhood street, we used those dime rubber balls from Schuman's. No bat. You hit with your fist. A manhole cover was home plate, first base was a tree by Mrs. Ireland's rooming house, and a light pole was second base. We didn't have a complete diamond. You'd run to first to second to home. We'd just choose up sides and play for hours.

The Pattersons, who lived next door, had a basket on their garage. I'd shoot baskets there, and eventually I developed a tradition. As soon as I was old enough for my parents to let me stay up until midnight on New Year's Eve, I'd run out in the cold (and sometimes in snow) just before the clock struck twelve. I'd take the last shot of the old year and then the first shot of the new year. Always, I'd make that first shot. Taking no chances, it would be a layup.

I attended South Avenue Grammar School, just a half mile from home. We walked, making the trip twice because we also came home for lunch. No school bus. No rides to school from parents in those days. And no concern by parents about the safety of their kids. My mother was always home when we got there for lunch. Usually I had my favorite, a peanut-butter-and-jelly sandwich. Dad also would come home for lunch. We ate meals as a family. Changes in society make lunch together impossible for most families, with kids eating at school cafeterias and parents eating at or near their places of employment. Many families unfortunately find it rare when they even can have dinner together.

We also often listened to the radio together for entertainment and for news. We laughed together at Jack Benny, George Burns and Gracie Allen, Amos and Andy, Abbott and Costello. We worried together over radio reports about the threat of another war, this time with Russia, with nuclear bombs. It was scary for children. For adults, too. After one frightening report about

aggressive moves by Russia, I remember offering a naïve suggestion based on grade school geography and a child's hope for
avoiding devastation: "If it's land Russia wants, we have all that
land in the Dakotas and Kansas and in Texas and the desert. I'm
sure we could work it out." Strength, not giving away land, was
of course the answer.

South Avenue Grammar was kindergarten through sixth
grade. On the sidewalk outside the school is where I kissed
Nancy Ferrell when we were in kindergarten. After grammar
school, I went on to Beacon Junior High School, seventh and
eighth grades. It was in the same building as the high school and
was just a little less than a half mile from home. Again, we walked.

In junior high I got my nickname. "Digger" isn't exactly a
common nickname, especially for a basketball coach. Even when
I worked for the first President Bush in the White House, everybody called me "Digger," and I wouldn't have wanted it any other
way. When I got a lot of publicity in coaching, especially after my
Notre Dame team broke that eighty-eight-game win streak of
mighty UCLA, stories about this upstart coach who was called
"Digger" explained that the name came because I was the son of
an undertaker. Although this seemed an adequate explanation, I
confess that there's a little more to the story.

Since the junior high was in the same building as the high
school, seventh- and eighth-grade boys who loved sports, as I did,
dreamed of sometime being a high school hotshot. Thus, we volunteered to be water boys for the varsity football team or batboys
for the baseball team. We'd travel around the Hudson Valley,
playing Poughkeepsie, Wappingers, Peekskill, and other rivals.

I was lucky enough to become the batboy. And on one trip,
I went back to the bus during batting practice and discovered
cupcakes and cookies the guys had for after-game snacks. Boy, did
they taste good.

Well, when I was growing up, there was a popular radio
(and then TV) program called *The Life of Riley*, a comedy about
a character named Chester A. Riley. Another character that
would drop in during the show to converse with Riley was named
Digby "Digger" O'Dell, "the friendly undertaker." He would re-

mark about something like having "covered a lot of ground today" and always depart with his best-known line, "I'd better be shoveling off."

Back on the bus after the game, the hungry players had no snacks but a sure knowledge of the culprit who took them. I had come back after batting practice with chocolate all over my face, proof of guilt. The players are threatening to impose instant justice, to knock the chocolate out of me. I'm yelling for the coach, Jim Gauriloff, to save me. Save me he did, but with a dire warning, "If you don't stop eating the team's cupcakes, I'm gonna put you in one of your old man's boxes. Do you understand, Digger O'Dell?" They laughed. They also remembered at the next game, hollering things like, "Hey, Digger O'Dell, where's my bat?" It stuck and finally was shortened to just "Digger."

As soon as I was old enough to ride a bicycle, I began to explore Beacon. Then, when we were a little older, my friends and I would explore beyond, riding to the river, the creek, the old factory sites, never with the dangers that lurk today in so many cities, small as well as large.

Those were great times in Beacon. I loved the place. Still do. And believe me, you can go home again. And should, again and again. While I returned to Beacon more often when my parents were alive, I go back still, always reminiscing about those fond times, meeting with lifelong friends and thinking about what I learned on the streets.

Hard times hit downtown Beacon in later decades, just as happened in so many of our cities. It was sad to see empty stores, to hear about dealers peddling drugs right downtown, to learn of gang activity, to receive warnings that my mother, living as a widow so close to a deteriorating downtown, could be in danger of violence. Now, when I return, it's great to see that the community is growing, a place popular as home for people commuting to New York City for their jobs. Downtown is flourishing again; stores that had been boarded up are renovated for new enterprises. Modern housing developments abound. A brand new multimillion-dollar high school is a great asset for Beacon.

It is recognized as a beacon again. It always was for me.

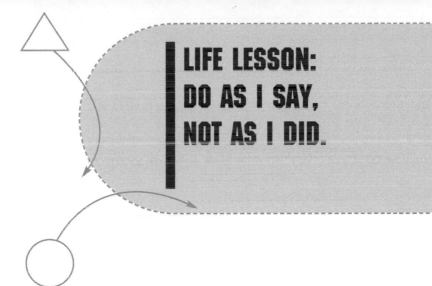

Chapter 6

Hail, Caesar

"There we were, five 'notorious' ringleaders of riot, appearing before Uncle Willie, hopeful but uncertain how he would respond to the accusations against us. Our fate was in his hands. Do we graduate? Can we take the Regents exams that must be passed in order to get a degree?

'You can take your exams,' Uncle Willie told us. 'If you pass, we're gonna let you graduate.'

He believed us, believed the truth that we hadn't planned to start riotous conduct."

Six

Although I stress today the importance of education, I must admit that my own high school academic career was, well . . . checkered. Being an undertaker's son was no help in learning a dead language, Latin. Nothing helped. And because a desk flew out a window, my graduation from Beacon High School in the spring of 1959 was in doubt. Now, there was no doubt about eventually graduating. My father would have demanded that I keep trying for a degree even if it had taken me ten tries to pass second-year Latin. It took me only five tries.

Veni, vidi, vici. I thought the translation was something like, "I came. I saw her. I winked." That made more sense to me. Gaul was divided into three parts. Big deal. But after translating that, I didn't care if the Belgs, whoever they were, lived in one part or that those Aquitanians had another part and the Gauls had the third part. I wanted no part of Latin.

For five semesters, including summer school, it was unfortunately a part of me. If I hadn't passed the New York Regents exam on the fifth try, I would have been in the same class with my sister Diane. Maybe that's what finally gave me the extra motivation to pass.

History I enjoyed, especially New York history, much of which I recall today, and U.S. and world history as well.

My best friend in high school was Normington Schofield Jr. With a name like that, a kid had to have a nickname. "Norm," most called him. My nickname for him was "Caesar." Our friendship developed not just from our participation on the junior high school and high school sports teams but also through our disdain for and inability to pass Latin. When Norm flunked the Regents Latin test repeatedly, too, "Caesar" it was.

Caesar went on to become a teacher, coach, and community leader in Beacon. Funny how so many of the guys who weren't exactly academic superstars in high school, some who often seemed like me to get in trouble, went on to successful careers. Lessons taught in families, in neighborhoods, in churches, and in the friendly rather than dangerous streets were as important as anything learned in the classroom.

The moral of this story of Caesar and me is not that high school doesn't matter. We did learn, even if not a lot of Latin. Instead, it could serve as a reminder to any kids with less than honor-roll grades today that you still can go on, as I did, to graduate from college, even get a master's degree, and then be hired at a place like Notre Dame.

Then there was that desk.

It was the desk of John Laing, my homeroom teacher. Boys and girls were separated in different homerooms back then at Beacon High. So it was all senior boys in Mr. Laing's room. For one reason or another, perhaps mostly because we were teenage boys rebelling against or at least questioning authority, we disliked taking directions from Mr. Laing. Maybe it was because he was an English and drama teacher, and we didn't find that macho. He was young and thin, hair kind of slicked back. We just didn't give him much respect, and we didn't think he respected us either. Today it could be described as a personality conflict. We thought we had all kinds of personality and wanted to show it off. He disagreed and objected.

Mr. Laing probably was a fine man and a good teacher. In fact, he did a very good job directing plays, including a play in which I had a part. By the spring of our senior year, the boys of Laing were ready to test authority as never before. Some of this was school tradition. Seniors, as the days to graduation approached, were known to skip some classes, with teachers not that concerned if the school subjects already had been mastered in preparation for the Regents tests.

A half dozen of us decided to go bowling one spring day, in the midst of a school day. We got back to Beacon High about three o'clock. And there she was, Mrs. Jane Way, a school matron who'd smack you on the arm as hard as she could and then ask why you weren't in a classroom. She got attention in her forceful way and asked what we were doing out of class. "Just coming back from bowling," we bragged. She didn't believe us. And neither did Mr. Laing, to whom we were reported. He just couldn't believe it until, proud of our excursion, we put the bowling sheets on his desk.

On the last day of classes, Mr. Laing issued what we took as a challenge. Some kid in the homeroom, just joking in a way to get his goat, said we might throw his desk out the window. "If you do that, I'll resign from teaching," he said. We looked at each other. We weren't contemplating *Hamlet*, but this offered a consummation devoutly to be wished.

After lunch, we staged a fight in the hall. Danny Curtin, now a lawyer and one of my best friends back home, was involved in the diversion, with kids yelling and screaming. Mr. Laing scampered to investigate.

Three of us opened the window—we had measured already for desk size—and hoisted the desk for a flight from the third level of our beautiful brick school.

Alas, Chuck Bradbury, a young physical education teacher we all liked, was right below in the parking lot. "Hey, Chuck, move over a little bit to your right," I shouted. He did but not quite enough. "A little bit more," I advised, motioning him out of danger. With Chuck safe, the desk wasn't. Out it went, crashing and smashing to pieces.

We fled to the school softball field. For the remainder of the afternoon, we played softball against the physical education classes that came to the field, one after another, for the final three periods of the day. We weren't too worried. Although cutting classes wasn't officially condoned, doing so on the last day of school was a tradition for seniors. We feared no harsh discipline.

When we came back to face some punishment for the flying desk, we figured even that wouldn't be severe. Heck, the desk was of little dollar value, and after all, we were in the exalted status of graduating seniors.

What we saw back at the school building, however, was shocking. There had been what the *Beacon News* was to report on page one as RIOT AT BEACON HIGH. We didn't plan it, didn't want it. Restlessness as the last day of school approached always triggered some student pranks. But a riot? The flying desk inspired conduct far beyond the prank definition.

Kids at the adjoining middle school, where tensions had been building because of an unpopular administrator, joined in with the unruly conduct of their high school elders. Paper littered the parking lot. Wastebaskets had been thrown out the window. Girls had turned on fire hoses. Water flowed in hallways that also echoed with the explosion of cherry bombs. Kids dropped the cherry bombs down toilets in the restrooms, resulting in thunderous noise, sounding like real explosives. What a mess.

The next day, two detectives came to our house. They sought a suspect—me—and hauled me off to the police station in a squad car for questioning. "Jesus, Mary, and Joseph!" my mother kept repeating, a prayer that this wayward son would not go to prison and also a plea to the Holy Family to keep him from riotous conduct in the future. "Glory be to God," she exclaimed, as I was taken away in most inglorious fashion.

Ronny Piccone, now a real estate guru, the Donald Trump of Beacon, was first on the detectives' hit list. I was second. They had the goods on us. Sort of. Except they assumed wrongly that we had done more than drop the desk, that we had sought to stage a riot.

"Where did you get the cherry bombs?" they interrogated.

We had none, had no plans for their use, had no idea why they became an explosive signal for kids to engage in "riot" conduct.

The cherry bombs, the authorities discovered, actually had been purchased by the Chandler Drum and Bugle Corps from Beacon on a trip to Florida for an Orange Bowl appearance. High school kids who were a part of the corps bought the cherry

bombs in South Carolina and Georgia. Since the Chandler director also was a school transportation director, authorities backed
away from trying to affix blame. We had no idea any kids were
planning—desk drop or not—to have some explosive fun as the
school year ended.

Fear of the detectives? Sure. It was scary for a high school
kid to be hauled in by the cops for questioning. But what I feared
most of all was my father's wrath. You think of whether the detectives will shine bright lights in your eyes and beat you with a
rubber hose. (They didn't.) If they had, however, it would have
been mild in comparison with what I expected to face from my
dad. With his temper, always triggered when I messed up in
school, I was sure that accusations of starting a school riot would
bring something like being tossed in the morgue at the funeral
home, either dead or wishing that I was.

But I was wrong. Dad's biggest concern was over whether I
would graduate. He was calm, cool, collected, and calculating a
defense that would build a case for graduating. To say the least,
he wasn't pleased with the desk caper, but he believed me when I
explained that I had no intention of starting a riot.

As I think back, I realize Dad's temper often was more
controlled than I imagined in my fears of a parental decision to
dump me for burial in one of the boxes stored upstairs at the
funeral home. Yes, he had a real temper. So do I. Well, I wasn't
always as irate at my players as I made it seem when they didn't
play defense or rebound. I didn't hate them. I didn't want them
buried. I sought motivation, not extermination. Same with
Dad.

The day after I became an entry on the police blotter, the
Beacon High School principal, Mr. William H. Pearse, known to
us fondly as "Uncle Willie," called the offending seniors for final
judgment on punishment, including whether we would be permitted to graduate.

Uncle Willie was a fine man, a distinguished grandfather
figure, with a fringe of white hair around his balding head. He always wore a suit and tie at school, always with a shirt with French
cuffs and cufflinks. At school assemblies where he spoke, the kids

gave him a standing ovation. He was beloved, as were some other teachers. Uncle Willie was fair, competent, and inspiring. Nobody ever thought of throwing Uncle Willie's desk out the window. If somebody did, I would have decked him. We loved Uncle Willie.

There we were, five "notorious" ringleaders of riot, appearing before Uncle Willie, hopeful but uncertain how he would respond to the accusations against us. Our fate was in his hands. Do we graduate? Can we take the Regents exams that must be passed in order to get a degree?

"You can take your exams," Uncle Willie told us. "If you pass, we're gonna let you graduate."

He believed us, believed the truth that we hadn't planned to start riotous conduct. "But we've got to do something as punishment," Uncle Willie told us. "You've gotta give something up." He couldn't let a desk be dropped out a window, sparking even unintentionally a riotous situation, without some very serious penalty.

I came up with a suggestion: "Well, what if you cancel the senior prom?" Wow. That sounded like a serious punishment for the senior class in response to the conduct of the senior boys of Laing.

Uncle Willie agreed to that punishment. And serious punishment it was—for the girls more than for the boys. We didn't mind cancellation of the prom. We welcomed it. The prom was a girl thing. We had to rent fancy clothes we hated to wear, buy flowers (except in my case, what with my father's business), take the girls to some expensive restaurant, and then waste time with some stupid dance steps watched by chaperones. For the girls, it was the opportunity to wear fancy gowns, receive pretty corsages, get taken to an elegant restaurant, and dance to dreamy music.

I was willing to take the hit in suggesting cancellation of the prom. I didn't have a date anyway. What a hit I took. The senior girls hated me. Word was out that Digger was the one who proposed sacrificing the prom as punishment. Some of the girls and their parents organized a dance outside school jurisdiction at St.

Rocco's Hall to take the place of the prom. It was by invitation only. I wasn't invited.

For our initial high school reunions, I stayed away. No sense going to face the wrath of angry women who still blamed me for destroying their prom. Finally, at the twenty-fifth reunion, I thought it was safe to attend, even though it was held at St. Rocco's Hall. Still, they remembered the demise of the prom. By then, however, they were laughing at what happened—at the alleged riot and the abandoned dance—rather than wanting to smite the prom destroyer.

Don't get the impression we didn't appreciate the efforts of the many fine teachers at Beacon High. One of the best was G. Richard Hewes, a history teacher who taught the subject in a way that made it interesting, vital. We gave Mr. Hewes the respect we accorded a priest. There was no nonsense in his class. Mrs. Flora MacNemar was a sweet lady. But there sometimes was nonsense in her class, even though we liked her. It's a wonder we didn't drive her nuts.

One of the honors of my high school years came when I was a junior. I was chosen to recite the Gettysburg Address at the Beacon Memorial Day observance. I was in suit and tie, standing almost at attention at the microphone, very serious and well aware of the significance of the occasion and of the words—a different Digger from the kid who tossed the desk.

While I played varsity baseball and junior varsity football and even went out for track my senior year, basketball was of course my best sport. I'd like to say that I was a star that led Beacon High to an undefeated season. Not so, however. For the 1958–59 season, my senior year, our hopes were high. There were exciting games, six decided by ten points or fewer. We lost five of those. We started out beating Middletown, 89–71, but then lost to Arlington by four points, to Roosevelt by two and to Peekskill in a terrible 72–33 trouncing.

Our record was five wins, eleven losses. I averaged in double figures, and my buddy Caesar did some terrific rebounding. Caesar and I played tough, physical defense for coach Mike Scoba. Nobody was saying, however, that "you're gonna hear about that Phelps kid in college basketball." Nobody.

What they did say about me in a poem by my senior class picture in the yearbook was this:

Tall, dark and handsome is our "Digger";
In his beautiful sweaters he cuts a sharp figure;
On the basketball court he shows his ability;
In his Father's profession he proves his agility.

Also in the yearbook was a feature listing some of the seniors and suggesting in my case: "Wouldn't it be strange to see . . . Richard Phelps . . . minus his strut." Wonder what they meant?

I got my diploma. Due to Latin and some other classes I didn't take seriously enough, my high school grade average wasn't very high. Some administrator once warned me that I was then 111th out of 113 in my graduating class. Probably just some attempt to motivate me. I never could have dropped that low. Right?

Chapter 7

The Judge Ruled

"We had fun, playing pranks on each other. I certainly was not immune to retaliation. And usually we didn't go too far, except for the time some of us were out on the lake with boats and water skis, pretending we were in a battle of PT boats, which involved tossing the seats that served as life preservers as though they were torpedoes.

'Normie,' a commanding voice called. 'You guys are on your way to becoming landlubbers for the rest of the vacation.' The judge ruled."

Seven

Off I went to Rider College in Trenton, New Jersey. There I would study business administration in preparation for joining my father in our family business. No more would I be just an undertaker's son. I'd be an undertaker. We had plans for expansion. My parents eventually bought land for a second funeral home, one I would manage. When Dad retired, I would take over the expanded enterprise, ready to do so with expertise from earning a business degree and then going on to graduate from Simmons Embalming School in Syracuse, where Dad learned his skills. Those were the plans. Time to get serious.

Well, more serious. I had a great time in high school, doing well in sports and in some classes I liked, especially history. Where I had neither interest nor incentive, I did just enough to get by—eventually, such as on that fifth try in Latin. Now, I advocate tougher high school requirements for the high-tech computer era and global competition. Lest anyone think I have been glamorizing just getting by in my own case, let me stress that my Beacon High School education provided the basics to go on to college, to graduate, and then to get a master's degree at Rider. I even got a doctorate. (Well, in all honesty I must note quickly that it was an honorary degree conferred when I delivered the commencement address at Rider. So I don't expect to be addressed as "Dr. Digger.")

In high school, I was taking college prep courses. I wasn't in warehousing classes of the type to which too many kids are relegated today. These are classes that provide no preparation for college or much of anything else.

Kids respond to challenge. I would have done better if the requirements had been tougher back then. I knew I'd graduate with the college preparatory courses I needed. When necessary, I'd come through. I had developed confidence that I could. And my parents were there to make sure that I did. Kids who drop out today are so often the ones who have no parental guidance, nobody to insist that they get a high school diploma and look ahead to college or some other postsecondary education or training.

Meanwhile, my closeness to death in our family business had already led to development of a philosophy of not wasting time while still there is life to live, to experience, to enjoy. There just didn't seem to be any reason to "waste" more time on academics than necessary to get a diploma, get to college, play some basketball there, and slip through to a degree in business administration, learn embalming, and return to Beacon to take care of the recently deceased.

Looking back, greater incentive could have been there if I had realized that higher grades were needed for an appointment to the U.S. Military Academy at West Point, so close along the Hudson River. When as kids we played football and pretended we were Johnny Lujack of Notre Dame or Doc Blanchard or Glenn Davis of Army, I thought then about going to Notre Dame—kind of far off, all the way out there in some state called Indiana. But I dreamed more of going to the close-to-home West Point. Somehow, I didn't understand, as so many kids don't, that poor grades in high school can shut the door on many college opportunities. Although less-than-impressive grades won't keep you from success, they can keep you from desired opportunities, like going to West Point.

Even at Rider, I couldn't let go of the possibility of attending a service academy. Instead of returning for the second semester of my freshman year, I went to Columbia Prep in Washington, D.C., then regarded as a preparatory school for the Naval Academy. I hated it. Man, was I homesick. For the first time in my life I was living in a place I didn't like.

"I'm coming home," I told my dad. "I'll go to junior college at home."

"No, you won't," he said in a tone that brought back memories of fear as a little kid that he'd dump me in one of his boxes. "Go back to Rider or go in the army," he offered as the choices. He didn't mean "Army" as in West Point, but "army" as in enlisting as a recruit for basic training in the infantry. Again, he knew when to get tough with me. And I knew the alternative to take. I finished the semester at Columbia Prep and went back to Rider.

Because of my need to catch up at Rider, I wound up taking twenty credit hours some semesters. When I had to buckle down, I could and did. In addition, I lettered in basketball my junior and senior years and in golf my senior year. While I didn't hit many baskets, I was described as a "fine defensive specialist." When you don't exactly have a Michael Jordan touch in shooting and aren't a powerful seven-footer, you'd better do all the "little things"— block out for rebounds, set a screen, take a charge, hound the other guy on defense—or else you will sit on the bench. Although I wasn't thinking then of ever coaching, learning those "little things" was vital preparation.

Despite an extra course load plus demands of basketball and golf, I also found time, as always, to have fun, especially after I pledged with Tau Kappa Epsilon. Our TKE fraternity at Rider was the original "Animal House." When the movie came out, I thought one of my fraternity brothers wrote it. We often partied and ended up on social probation. We sometimes were obnoxious. We pulled pranks. There was the time a brother tattled on us for joking around during our mandatory study hall, and we retaliated by hoisting his Volkswagen up on the front porch. We "borrowed" a Buddha figure from a miniature golf course, painted it in TKE colors and declared it our mascot for flag football games.

But we also bonded and worked together to win most of the time in fraternity competition, whether in flag football or decorating for homecoming. We were a diverse group, including the first black to pledge, and we helped each other overcome our own weaknesses simply by making fun of all of our flaws. We didn't snap at each other and then sulk. We ridiculed each other, often with cutting humor, and laughed about it. As much as we snared each other with verbal harpoons, we came together to win whenever it was Us vs. Them.

Although Notre Dame doesn't have fraternities and does well without them, there was a little TKE in my basketball teams. In chewing out a player for lack of effort or mistakes, I'd often use the TKE type of barb to make a point with humor and ridicule. Players could get on each other for team betterment, bonding for the contest of Us vs. Them.

When I was asked one year during my Notre Dame coaching career to head the annual alumni fund drive at Rider, Dr. Frank Elliott, then Rider president, told me that the TKE house in the 1958–1964 era, my era, had a more impressive array of highly successful graduates than was found in any other house on campus ever. I couldn't help but laugh. The Animal House? Of course. We were preparing each other, in our own prodding way, for the success achieved by our alums, those who went on to be winners—mayors of their cities, chief executives of their firms, top salespersons in their fields, and leaders of civic and charitable endeavors in their communities.

While I don't want to provide even a smidgen of suggestion that academics are not important, I strongly believe that the value of college includes the association with others, hopefully a diverse group—from other states, other countries, other races, other religions, other economic status, and making friendships that last a lifetime.

Speaking of lasting friendships, my friend Caesar, a.k.a. Normington Schofield Jr., and I maintained our friendship as we went on to different colleges and eventually to live in different parts of the country and to pursue different activities. When we were in college, we would go in the summer to his family's place on Long Lake at Harrison, Maine. His dad was a judge. We called him "Big Caesar." His little brother was "Little Caesar." His mother, Mary Schofield, was known as "Bulla." And the guys who would get together at the lake called the place "Bulla's Training Camp for Boys." She made sure we had plenty to eat, and we made sure we were running to get in shape for our sports, even if we often had a car follow with a couple of beers to cool off after the run.

Sometimes we'd be up kind of late. But the judge liked to go out on the lake early for fishing. At about five in the morning, he'd knock on the door of the room where we bunked at the cottage and yell, "Normie, come on. We're goin' fishin' now." The last thing wanted by Caesar, a.k.a. Normie, was to wake up, get up, and go out on the lake. "Ya gotta go," I'd tell him. "It's Big Caesar." Off he would go, not as much interested in catching fish as he was in catching more sleep.

Once when he had just climbed back into bed, Bulla called up, "Normie, you want anything to eat?" I could disguise my voice to sound like Caesar, so I mumbled back, "Yeah, Mom, three eggs over easy." No way he wanted to face three over-easy eggs looking up at him.

Another time when we were up at the lake getting the place ready for Caesar's sister's wedding, Caesar was on the phone talking to a girl back in Beacon that he really liked, Helene, his high school sweetheart. We always teased him about Helene. Well, the guys working on getting the cottage fixed up had been drinking as well as fixing. There was a huge pyramid of beer cans on a table. "Come on, Caesar, we gotta go," I hollered, trying once more to get him finally off the phone. Still he talked, repeating to Helene how much he missed her.

"Here's how much he really misses you," I shouted into the phone, tipping over the table and sending the beer cans crashing. Helene hangs up. Caesar starts shouting at me for ruining his romance. But I knew better. "Don't worry about it," I told him. "She still loves you." She did. This was a high school romance that resulted in a very happy marriage.

We had fun, playing pranks on each other. I certainly was not immune to retaliation. And usually we didn't go too far, except for the time some of us were out on the lake with boats and water skis, pretending we were in a battle of PT boats, which involved tossing the seats that served as life preservers as though they were torpedoes.

"Normie," a commanding voice called. "You guys are on your way to becoming landlubbers for the rest of the vacation." The judge ruled.

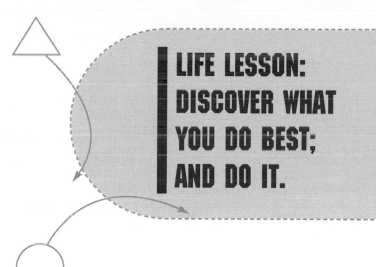

Chapter 8

My Most Important Game

"During the game, I wasn't even on the bench to help with coaching. As a volunteer assistant, my job that day was to be the analyst for the radio station that broadcast the Rider games. While I don't remember a thing I pontificated in that analysis, believe me, a tape of that broadcast was not offered when I got my job as an analyst with ESPN. Still today, however, I remember exactly my thoughts after that game: 'I can do this.' Back at my apartment, I kept thinking of that four-word conclusion: 'I can do this.' That led to a decision: 'I will do this.'

No Simmons School of Embalming. No undertaking back with the family business in Beacon. Rather, a new undertaking, coaching. I had an objective, a dream."

Eight

After graduation from Rider, I was back in Beacon in that summer of '63, helping with funerals and preparing to head off to Simmons School of Embalming, where I would spend a year and then take the state exam to get a license as an embalmer and funeral director.

Meanwhile, Tom Winterbottom had been hired as a new basketball coach at Beacon High. After going 20–0 his first year, Tom started a summer basketball league. Under state rules, he couldn't coach his own Beacon players in the league, so he asked me if I would coach the team.

"Sure," I said. "But you gotta teach me everything about coaching." Me? A coach? Never thought about doing that. Soon, I could think of nothing else.

Tom talked to me for hours about offense and defense. He gave me a book on basketball theory. I devoured it in one night. I liked coaching. And I recalled one time when I was in college and was back home teaching a bunch of younger kids some basketball techniques at the church across the street from our home. The minister, who had been watching, said, "You know, you should be a coach." Didn't think about what he said then. Now, I did.

Coaching was what I wanted to do, at least to try. I didn't want to go to Simmons and then embalm and bury. I told my parents that I wanted to try something else, at least to put off going to Simmons. They were great. They also were disappointed, I knew. But to this day I thank them, now in prayer for their souls, for letting me do what I really wanted. Dad was tough on me when I was about to make a dumb decision, such as slip back to a junior college instead of returning to Rider, but he was always with me when I needed encouragement, a chance. "Go do what you want to do," he told me.

Coach? Where? I inquired at Beacon High if I could teach there and be an assistant coach. They laughed. They looked at my class standing when I graduated. Yep, another reminder that grades are important. I could find no high school job anywhere. Thus, I made another decision, one of many of the type that you look back on as fortuitous. I would go back to Rider to get a master's degree in business education. The kid who didn't take well to academics would seek an advanced degree, which I knew would be helpful in seeking the college coaching position to which I would one day aspire. I also would be a volunteer basketball assistant at Rider.

My dad kept for a time the land he had purchased for our planned new funeral home. Actually, he had picked a great location in which there was tremendous growth. Lots of potential customers. My parents thought that going for that master's degree in business education would be of considerable value when I came to my senses and went into a business that always has customers rather than into coaching this uncertain dribbling stuff.

On March 3, 1964, Rider was the David playing Goliath—New York University, then one of the national powers in basketball. NYU was going to the National Invitational Tournament, at that time a premier tournament. Rider was going nowhere. NYU had a powerful team led by Harold "Happy" Hairston, who would go on to NBA fame as a star for the Los Angeles Lakers, and Barry Kramer, a future NBA player who then was touted by many sportswriters as the best college player in the country. Height was provided at center by Ray "Big Ben" Bennett.

Most challenging of all was that we were to play NYU at what was then its home-campus court, Alumni Gymnasium at University Heights in the Bronx. NYU had not lost a game there in twenty-three years, not since a 1941 loss to Penn State. This was kind of like David not even having a slingshot.

As a volunteer assistant coach, I scouted Goliath, watching NYU play Iona and Hofstra. "We can beat these guys," I told Coach Bob Greenwood. "Here's how."

Brash? Hey, why do some people insist I'm brash? To me, it was just stating a fact. Coach Greenwood, who had come to appreciate my interest in basketball strategy and coaching, let me put in my game plan over two days of practice. He wasn't just writing off the game as hopeless by letting a young assistant devise some perhaps nutty scheme. After Greenwood evaluated my scouting reports and my game plan, he believed that it just might work. We sold it to the team, and that was vital. A good game plan in which players have no confidence can bring defeat. The plan and the confidence both need to be strong to pull an upset.

A key part of my game plan against NYU was using a sixth man, a strategy I was to perfect and employ often in pulling upsets of seven No. 1 teams while coaching against various Goliaths at Notre Dame. Six men? Not in the Rider lineup, of course. We counted on one of the NYU players to help us. In this case it was "Big Ben" Bennett. I detected in scouting that the towering Bennett was trouble for opponents under the basket, but he didn't hit when he took shots from out a ways and then didn't follow up to rebound his miss. Thus, my strategy was to leave him open away from the basket, concentrate defense on the other four NYU players and actually encourage "Big Ben" to stay and shoot away from the basket.

David won. Final score: Rider, 66; NYU, 63.

We led by only a point with twenty-nine seconds left. Then Dick Kuchen, a Rider player who was to go on to be one of my finest assistants at Notre Dame and then to be a head college coach, sank two free throws for the final margin.

Our defense worked. "Big Ben" scored only eight points. Hairston and Kramer got their points, as we knew they would, but just nineteen each rather than higher totals that would have ended our upset bid.

During the game, I wasn't even on the bench to help with coaching. As a volunteer assistant, my job that day was to be the analyst for the radio station that broadcast the Rider games. While I don't remember a thing I pontificated in that analysis, believe me, a tape of that broadcast was not offered when I got my job as an analyst with ESPN. Still today, however, I remember exactly my thoughts after that game: "I can do this." Back at my apartment, I kept thinking of that four-word conclusion: "I can do this." That led to a decision: "I will do this."

No Simmons School of Embalming. No undertaking back with the family business in Beacon. Rather, a new undertaking, coaching. I had an objective, a dream. In looking at the decades of life, this is the time, the age of twenty-something, to decide on a dream and chase it. Right then, I knew my dream was to be a college basketball coach and that I would chase it and try as best I could to catch it.

The dream doesn't have to be something in sports—shouldn't be, couldn't be for most young people. The dream can be to become a successful designer of homes or clothes or Web pages; to be a lawyer, a carpenter, a doctor, a plumber, an architect, a chef, a pilot, or, yes, a funeral director. Something useful. Something that would be rewarding. Something that wouldn't be drudgery. There is a need for some goal for which to strive. Maybe it won't be reached. Certainly it won't be reached, however, if there is no striving. Coming close to a goal also can be rewarding. Surpassing, also possible, is even better.

Nobody asks me today about the most important basketball game of my life. The assumption is that obviously it was that famed 71–70 Notre Dame victory to snap UCLA's record winning streak in 1974.

Wrong. The most important game of my life was that Rider upset of NYU in 1964. If my game plan had fizzled, if "Big Ben" had chimed in loudly with twenty points, if NYU had trounced Rider, I could have been headed for Simmons instead of Notre Dame. If not for that game convincing me that "I can do this," I might well have been directing a funeral on January 19, 1974, rather than directing Notre Dame to that upset of UCLA.

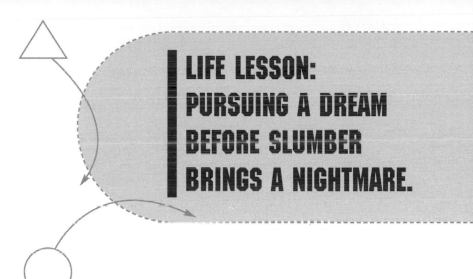

Chapter 9

Dreaming of Notre Dame

"Just as important as what you know is getting known and making sure those who will make decisions about your future are aware of your knowledge, skill, and goals. A young lawyer is nuts if he or she does not seek contacts at a prestigious law firm, if that is the goal. A junior executive is stupid not to try to get known by the CEO or chairman of the board. A salesperson should get out word of desire to be assigned to a bigger, better territory. An auto mechanic can let it be known that a goal is to become part owner of and eventually to run an auto shop."

Nine

Now I had my goal: to be a college basketball coach. But how would I reach it? Where would I start? It all started at Junior High School No. 4 in Trenton. I taught business math and typing and coached the downtrodden basketball team. My choice of jobs, with prospects so slim, could not be based on finding a basketball power. What I needed was just to find a job, a paycheck, while I still helped out at Rider. Junior High No. 4 had lost every game the prior season, going 0–8. The power in Trenton was Junior High No. 5, where years later I was to accompany Vice President Dan Quayle for his potato(e) mashing.

We lost our first four games. Then, enhancing my belief that "I can do this," I got the kids organized and enthused enough to win two in a row. I told them we were undefeated—the first part of the season didn't count. During one of our victories, the principal stopped by our gym partway through the game. We were winning by fifteen points. The principal, unaccustomed to seeing anything like that, admonished the student posting the points on the hand-operated scoreboard: "You got it backwards. You've got us ahead. It's supposed to be the visitors with the most points."

During the spring of that school year, I wrote to ten college basketball coaches, seeking a full-time assistant's job. Figuring I'd start at the top, I wrote to Coach Dean Smith at North Carolina. No luck. He hired instead a guy named Larry Brown. I couldn't get a college job anywhere, top or bottom. So when I heard of an opening for head coach at St. Gabriel's High School in Hazleton,

Pennsylvania, I applied and was hired by Father Ray Deviney and Father Joe Comboy, priests with a strong faith in God. They even had faith, though I'm not sure how strong, that I could coach at their school. Although it was at the high school level, here was a chance to get some head coaching experience at a small Catholic school that played some of the bigger schools. And I would put in the dominating press I envisioned my teams using on defense for the entire game.

Years later when I saw the classic movie *Hoosiers*, about a new coach who guides a tiny school to the Indiana high school basketball championship, one of the scenes just brought chills. It was the portrayal by Gene Hackman, in the role of the coach, of being warned by townspeople that their teams just didn't play the way he was teaching the boys. Exactly the same reaction greeted the new coach at St. Gabriel's.

"You wanna press? For a whole game? All four quarters? The team is gonna be exhausted. The boys are gonna foul out," they warned. "We don't press the whole game. None of the teams around here do that. You don't press unless you're in the fourth quarter and you're down by twelve."

"I'd rather press at the start of the game and be up twelve points in the first quarter," I told them. We pressed all game and went on to win the Class C Catholic state championship. While *Hoosiers* portrayed the team as well as the townspeople as being disgruntled over the strategy of a new coach, the kids at St. Gabriel's were great from the start.

Any head coach, no matter what the level of play, will find some fans and some relatives of players who believe they know better how to coach the team. If you know what you're doing, the players will understand, perform, and win. Through their success, they'll bring along most of the critics—though never all of those "experts."

While at St. Gabriel's, I wrote a letter, postmarked in Hazleton on October 30, 1965, to Ara Parseghian, the renowned football coach at Notre Dame. I told Parseghian of my love for Notre Dame and my goal of someday being the head basketball coach of the Irish. Six years later, at age twenty-nine, I was.

Brash? Probably so, considering I was then a first-year high school coach. But I was just citing a goal and hoping to get my name known at Notre Dame. Well, I achieved the goal, and when I arrived at Notre Dame, Ara became both a friend and a mentor, guiding me in becoming a member of the Notre Dame family and helping me with contacts nationally, even the contact with a future president of the United States whose administration I would join.

Next came the assistant coach's job at the college level that I needed. For four years I was an assistant coach at the University of Pennsylvania with Coach Dick Harter, whose teams tore up the Ivy League.

In seeking a goal—and mine was to coach at Notre Dame—more than just doing a good job usually is involved. This often is not understood by young people starting out on a career and striving for advancement. Networking can make the difference. It did for me. Notre Dame didn't hire me because my press worked at St. Gabriel's or due to my successful recruiting and assistant coaching at Penn. Now, obviously, if St. Gabriel's hadn't won a game or if I had done a poor job as an assistant at Penn, moving on to become a college head coach would not have been likely. But to move up to Notre Dame, I had to make contacts, to get known by the right people at Notre Dame and to get them to understand my burning desire to coach there.

There's nothing wrong with making contacts, with networking. Make acquaintances. Make friends among people who can help through exchange of information, maybe a tip on an upcoming job opening or advancement possibility. They also may be able to put in a good word for you where it counts. It's reciprocal. I've helped many a young coach for whom I have high regard to land a head coaching position or move to a more prestigious program. Still do.

Just as important as what you know is getting known and making sure those who will make decisions about your future are aware of your knowledge, skill, and goals. A young lawyer is nuts if he or she does not seek contacts at a prestigious law firm, if that is the goal. A junior executive is stupid not to try to get known by the CEO or chairman of the board. A salesperson should get out word of desire to be assigned to a bigger, better territory. An auto mechanic can let it be known that a goal is to become part owner of and eventually to run an auto shop.

A person doing a fine job still can be overlooked for advancement if the boss doesn't even realize there is desire to move to a more advanced position or if some other aspirant, though less qualified, has made a better impression through personal contacts. There is no need to be bashful about goals and achievements. Don't assume everybody already knows your qualifications. As the late Ray Madden, a longtime congressman from Gary, Indiana, used to say in stressing the need to remind others of your achievements: "He who does not toot his own horn has his horn untooted."

While still a Penn assistant, and only twenty-seven years old, I made a key contact. I was seeking to reach anyone who might be able to help me be considered when Johnny Dee retired as Notre Dame head coach. There had been rumors that Dee would retire in a couple of years, probably right after the graduation of Austin Carr, the outstanding player who still holds Notre Dame scoring records. No time to waste. Brash to think I could move up that fast? Yes. But that's what I wanted to do. So why not try?

Through a friend, I made contact with Johnny Druze, who had been a legendary football player before I was born. He was a member of the "Seven Blocks of Granite," the famed Fordham University line that also included Vince Lombardi. The reason I sought to talk with Druze had nothing to do with Fordham. He had been an assistant football coach at Notre Dame and still had campus contacts. I told him of my respect for Notre Dame and my desire to coach there. And I asked for any help he could provide. Druze provided more help than I had envisioned, in a way I never expected.

No opening yet at Notre Dame in 1970. Dee was set to coach Carr, generally regarded as the best player in the country, for the All-American's senior season. Suddenly, however, there was an opening at Fordham. Johnny Druze sold Pete Carlesimo, then the athletic director there, on considering me for head coach. Carlesimo, the father of successful college and pro coach P. J. Carlesimo, had been a football teammate of Johnny's at Fordham. I interviewed, was hired, and went on to a highly successful season at Fordham, including a victory over Carr and Notre Dame. And after that season, at twenty-nine, I was hired at Notre Dame to replace Dee, who had indeed resigned after the close of Carr's career. My networking was just as important as my game plan against Notre Dame, although the two became intertwined.

As a Penn assistant recruiting in Illinois and Indiana in 1968, I took a side trip to visit Notre Dame and have lunch with Moose Krause, the athletic director. This was my first visit to Notre Dame. Even though I learned as a little kid the words of the Victory March—probably before I learned the alphabet—and had followed the Fighting Irish football fortunes from as far back as I could remember, I never before had set foot on the campus.

Seeing the Golden Dome was a dream come true. By then, of course, my dream was not just to visit Notre Dame but to coach there. Dream I did while driving in on a back road (now I know it's called Juniper Road) toward the campus. As I passed a beautiful house by a stream, I fantasized to myself, "That's the house I'll buy." I didn't. Still, starting even to pick out a house shows how determined I was in pursuit of my goal.

All of a sudden, there was the campus, there were the buildings, and, my God, there to my right was Notre Dame Stadium. I parked and walked to the stadium, "the House that Rockne built." Thoughts went back to all those games I played as a kid in Beacon when I called myself Johnny Lujack, pretending to be the Irish quarterback. Here was where the real Lujack played, where all the other Fighting Irish football greats played.

A gate was open, and nobody was there to block entry. Shocking. I expected armed guards to be there to protect this shrine. There was a ramp. Up that ramp I hurried, still fearing somebody would shout that I had to leave. There was the field. There was the press box. Below it on that side, I knew, had to be the Notre Dame bench. Down to the field I went. There was the tunnel where the players raced onto the field to that most famous of all fight songs. Even at the TKE house, we played the Victory March at our flag football games.

With tears in my eyes and chills running down my spine, I could almost hear the voice of Bill Stern, the top radio sportscaster of my youth, doing his play-by-play account with dramatic flair: "Notre Dame is out of huddle. Into the T-formation. Time running out in the half, running out for the Irish on this drive. Lujack is back. Back to pass. He looks long. No. He throws over the middle to Leon Hart. Hart at the 20, to the 10. . . ,"

My enthusiasm was boundless when I had lunch with Moose Krause, a colorful figure who had been an All-American in football as well as basketball at Notre Dame. Moose was a wonderful man. He understood the sincerity of my desire to coach at Notre Dame. Eventually, he was in my corner when the time came for selection of a new coach. Then he became a supportive boss, never exhibiting the ego-driven micromanagement found in some athletic directors but always watchful to make sure we represented Notre Dame honestly and proudly.

Also in my corner in a very helpful way was Moose's secretary, Eleanor Van Der Hagen. While I was keeping in contact with Moose, Eleanor came to understand my passion to coach at Notre Dame, to sympathize, and finally to help me. Before my Fordham team played Notre Dame at Madison Square Garden, I scouted the Irish in their game with Marquette in Milwaukee. When I called Eleanor to tell her I would be in Milwaukee and hoped to make additional Notre Dame contacts, she arranged a contact that was to be instrumental in my eventual hiring. Eleanor called Marquette and got me seated on press row beside Roger Valdiserri, Notre Dame's superb sports information director. I had never before met him. But while I was scouting Notre Dame, Roger was scouting me as a potential Irish coach. He was to become my ace behind the scenes in the selection process.

I talked with Roger and Druze at the Garden just before our game with Notre Dame. With Roger's promise not to rush to tell Dee—and it would have been too late anyway for Notre Dame to change its game plan at tip-off—I explained how we could neutralize Carr and win with a zone we had not attempted all year. It worked. And Roger was becoming convinced. He sent Jim Gibbons, another Notre Dame official who was involved with athletics and other projects as well over a distinguished career, to evaluate our Fordham team and my coaching in our next Garden game, against Al McGuire's Marquette team. We lost but in overtime.

Valdiserri and Gibbons were instrumental in convincing Rev. Edmund P. Joyce to hire me. Joyce, the beloved Father Ned, was the executive vice president at Notre Dame with the final say on coaching decisions.

Maybe my high regard for that wonderful lady who was Moose's secretary, Eleanor Van Der Hagen, is one of the reasons I take an interest in people I meet who don't happen to be big-time coaches, big-name players, big-shot TV types, big-money business executives or big-mouth politicians. She was "just" a secretary. No, she was so much more, doing so much for Notre Dame, so much for me, for my dream, for my career.

Take time to talk with a secretary, with the guy who's bagging groceries, with a receptionist, with your waiter or waitress or repairman. Not because they may then do something to help you, although you never know. It's the right thing to do. Don't be a snob. My parents stressed that. And you may find some interesting things in conversation with folks you could brush off as not very important.

Each year back in Beacon at a charity golf event and at hockey great Mario Lemieux's celebrity invitational tournament in Pittsburgh, I see many of the same volunteers year after year. I get to know them by name. I'll joke with them and ask how things have been going. Sometimes not well. Perhaps I'll hear about the illness or death of a spouse. And there is appreciation that someone asked, that someone listened, that someone cared. Sometimes there is an achievement of a child or grandchild. Perhaps a big job, a big graduation day, or just a big game in Little League. And there is pride in being able to tell the details. Sometimes, there is a very interesting story. And I never would have heard of these happenings if I didn't ask.

At one Lemieux tournament, where there were celebrities such as Michael Jordan, Lou Holtz, John Elway, and, of course, Mario, the person I enjoyed renewing acquaintance with as much as anyone was "Moonshine Jack." Nobody else calls him that. His name is Jack Scott. He's been a volunteer for years at the fifth tee. Since he's from West Virginia, I'd joked with him before about stories of moonshine consumption there. This time he brought me a jug labeled "Digger's Moonshine Medicine." It was the real stuff. Drink it? Are you kidding? I left it with the guys who work at the bar at the club at Nevillewood.

You never know what you'll miss if you don't talk with people you meet. I could have missed everything from a key contact for a head coaching job at Notre Dame to a jug of moonshine.

Chapter 10

A Dream Comes True

"We played by the rules. Never a recruiting scandal. Never a problem with the NCAA. We recruited the right way, always, even when it meant losing a promising player who was swayed by promises from one of those colleges that do things the wrong way. We had no slush fund. No phantom courses offering credit without attendance. No phantom jobs offering pay without work. And our players won. On the court as well as in the classroom."

Ten

When I met with Father Joyce for my job interview, it wasn't at Notre Dame. We met at the Detroit airport. Roger Valdiserri called to tell me Notre Dame was announcing Johnny Dee's retirement on April 30, 1971, the Saturday after the NCAA tournament, and that Father Joyce wanted a secret rendezvous out of town, with both of us flying to Detroit to avoid news media scrutiny.

After our successful season at Fordham, with a top-ten finish, I was considered a hot prospect for several other head-coaching jobs, but Notre Dame was the one I wanted. When I asked Father Joyce what he expected of the next head coach, he cited three goals: "Graduate your players, never get in trouble with the NCAA, and be competitive." How competitive? "About eighteen wins a year," he said.

The Notre Dame salary offer of $18,000 a year for four years was far less than the $35,000 a year for contracts of similar length offered by Penn and Virginia Tech. No matter. After my meeting with Father Joyce, I was pretty certain I'd get the job I wanted most. He took the decision to the Athletic Board. Roger called to tell me it was a lock. So it was. My dream, expressed six years before in that letter to Ara Parseghian, had become reality. Ara still had that letter in his files, although I'm not claiming that he saved it due to expectation that I'd really wind up joining him as an Irish head coach. When I did, Ara was a big help, a mentor in the ways of Notre Dame and in handling the national attention the university attracts. And for twenty years I was the head basketball coach at Notre Dame, complying with the requirements stressed by Father Joyce.

We played by the rules. Never a recruiting scandal. Never a problem with the NCAA. We recruited the right way, always, even when it meant losing a promising player who was swayed by promises from one of those colleges that do things the wrong way. We had no slush fund. No phantom courses offering credit without attendance. No phantom jobs offering pay without work. And our players won. On the court as well as in the classroom.

My coaching record at Notre Dame was 393–197, which figures out to an average of just under twenty wins a year. Not bad, when you consider that the talent-thin team I inherited won only six games in my first year. Also, there was the handicap in my final couple of seasons of new athletic administrators and a new university president becoming a hindrance, not a help. They took over scheduling and messed it up in a way that curtailed chances of winning. They rejected all that I sought for the program, including my recommendation to join the Big East Conference. Successful recruiting for an independent basketball program had become as likely as survival by any other dinosaur. That was later acknowledged when the Irish did join the Big East, and it has improved recruiting opportunities for the program.

We were selected for the NCAA Tournament fourteen times and reached the Final Four in 1978. Also, we exceeded even the expectations of Father Joyce for a high graduation percentage. It was 100 percent. Can't get any higher than that. All fifty-six players who played four years for me received their degrees.

Enthusiasm for basketball grew at Notre Dame and enthusiasm grew nationally for our team. Our pep rallies before big games were crowded, loud, exciting—rivaling the atmosphere at the famed Notre Dame football rallies. Students cheered at the ACC with the same passion as their exaltations on a fall Saturday afternoon at the stadium. The ACC, which in some recent seasons has been relatively quiet, was back then a house of horrors for visiting teams.

Television coverage for our upset of UCLA, breaking their eighty-eight-game streak, was nationwide, thanks to the innovative efforts of Eddie Einhorn, now one of the principal owners of the Chicago White Sox along with Jerry Reinsdorf. Eddie was founder of TVS Television Network, the leading syndicator of sports programming in the 1970s. He helped attract fans to college basketball with a prime-time telecast of the UCLA vs. Houston game (Lew Alcindor vs. Elvin Hayes) in 1968 at the Astrodome. A big leap in national attention and popularity came when Eddie got our 71–70 thriller over UCLA on in every major market nationally in 1974.

Eddie wrote a book recently, *How March Became Madness: How the NCAA Tournament Became the Greatest Sporting Event in America*. He played a key role in the expanding popularity of college basketball. Now there's a national obsession with tournament pools, with people in offices all over America making picks—sometimes based on power ratings, sometimes just on favorite uniform colors—and following the results in all the brackets. Excitement builds as pairings are announced and then analyzed on TV, in the newspapers, and around the water cooler. TV ratings are solid. With all the interest in coverage, my ESPN colleague Dick Vitale has become the icon for college basketball.

Notre Dame, featured on TV more than any other team in the 1970s, also played a key role in the rising national interest. Eddie's advice was helpful to me in this as he suggested how to schedule with an eye toward attracting TV coverage and, thus, the attention that fueled interest in Notre Dame basketball and helped recruiting.

When we came to South Bend, we were a family of five. While in graduate school at Rider, I had met Teresa Godwin, a student who was the homecoming queen. She was warned by her sorority sisters about our TKE reputation for conduct of the type later immortalized in *Animal House*.

"Don't go out with Digger," they advised. "He's crazy." Kind of harsh. Later success of so many in that TKE house—animal or not—seems to disprove the evaluation. But I had provided ammunition for a critical view.

Terry and I were married. And early in our marriage we moved frequently as I changed coaching jobs and we sought larger homes for a growing family. Our move to South Bend was our fifth move in fourteen months. Our children were little: Karen was six; Rick, four; and Jen, two.

We didn't buy that house by the stream that I spotted on my first visit to Notre Dame. Couldn't have afforded it. Anyway, we found something better—the house in which I still live today, just two blocks from Notre Dame, in a very nice neighborhood with very nice neighbors. The best neighbor of all is Notre Dame, with all the places I love to visit, with what to me is sacred ground. South Bend is and will remain my home. Initially, we picked the house not just because of proximity to Notre Dame but also because it is close to St. Joseph's High School, where our kids would attend.

Terry also took advantage of being near Notre Dame. She had not completed work on her college degree when we were married and began all of our moving to different jobs. She obtained three degrees at Notre Dame—bachelor's, master's, and Ph.D.—and also a master's at Yale Law School. She began teaching legal writing at Notre Dame in 1980 and now is a professor regarded as one of the nation's foremost experts on legal writing.

We had a great family life, taking fun trips and enjoying life and success as the kids grew. One summer we vacationed in Canada, camping out. We were roughing it—or at least to me it was roughing it—what with cooking oatmeal and feasting on Kraft macaroni and cheese. Rick and I went for a walk and came across this gas station–restaurant place. We snuck in and, despite the roughing-it mode we were supposed to be observing, we gobbled down a few cheeseburgers. We went back to camping out, not mentioning the cheeseburger caper to the rest of the family. Then, on the last night there, Terry said we'd had enough oatmeal and macaroni and would go to a restaurant. We did. The same place where Rick and I had ventured earlier. The same guy who had served us was there.

"Hey, coach," he shouted. "Want another cheeseburger?" We were dead.

Another summer when I went to conduct a basketball clinic in Yugoslavia, I took the family along so that we could travel also to other countries in Europe. In Paris Terry was talking about our plans to see the Arc d'Triomphe. Rick, then fourteen and thinking of food other than what we had been eating in Europe, chimed in: "There's only one arch I wanna see, and it better be golden."

On a trip to Florence and Venice, we stayed in hostels. One bathroom. Not exactly places where you find a mint on the pillow, a newspaper at the door, or any of the other frills we get accustomed to in hotels in this country. Poor Jen, about twelve, was carrying a backpack, like the rest of us. Kind of heavy. Also it was hot. No air conditioning. But mosquitoes would blitz if the windows were opened. Finally, when we got to Switzerland, I proclaimed for the sake of Jen and the other kids: "We're going to a hotel, with air conditioning and showers, and I ain't worried about the cost." Certainly I was not a bit concerned about my own comfort; just decided to do it for the family.

In 1996, Terry and I were growing apart, going in different directions, and were divorced. Divorce is ugly. It's hell. It means the end of the family going on those vacations together, celebrating Christmas together, enjoying successes together, facing the problems of life together. It affects children, no matter what their age, sometimes terribly.

But divorce came. I didn't want it. But it happened, inevitably perhaps, as our lives took us on different paths. Terry was on an academic path, a successful one, and seeking more of a private life than I was pursuing. I had political ambitions, a desire to seek an office where there is no privacy, the presidency, because I thought I could make a difference.

When I said in an interview in the *Poughkeepsie Journal* early in 1995 that I was "angling for 2004" for a presidential candidacy, the story was picked up nationally. The *South Bend Tribune* phoned Terry in London, where she was spending a semester teaching in the Notre Dame law program. She had some funny comments. "And they thought Hillary was something," she quipped. "Wait 'til they get me."

But she also said, "I'm not packing for the White House yet." Nor would she ever, she told me in a way that included no funny quips. "You're not gonna do that to me," she said. "You're not gonna do that to the kids. We're not gonna go through that." She knew how everything in the private lives of presidential candidates becomes public. How there is no privacy. We were indeed looking down different paths, going in different directions. Finally, unfortunately, it became too late for us to turn back.

During my coaching years at Notre Dame, I'd still get back to Beacon and to Maine for summertime visits with Caesar. The visits were a little more subdued than in our college days. They were more family events, with Terry and me and our three kids joining Caesar and Helene and their four kids.

One summer, after all the pressure of the season and then some frustrating recruiting, I was wound really tight, in need of relaxation. But I was finding it difficult to relieve the stress and get into a relaxed mood. Caesar figured I'd relax a bit with some bass fishing on Crystal Lake, next to Long Lake, where their place was located. Sounded like a good idea.

Within thirty seconds after Caesar began to fish, he landed a nice bass. Then he caught another fish and another and another. Not a bite for the hook on my line. This was not relieving stress.

"How the hell are you doin' that?" I asked. "Are we using the same bait?" We were, despite my suspicion that my hook offered something about as pleasing to the fish as that roughing-it diet of oatmeal and macaroni had been for me. Then Caesar caught another big fish.

"What's goin' on here?" I demanded. "It's got to be the pole. You've got a better pole. Let me have that pole." Caesar, such a kind guy trying to help me settle down, agreed to trade poles. And darned if he didn't right away catch a fish with my pole.

Some guys from a nearby camp came past in a boat, and I yelled at them for coming into our space. "Come on, Digger, you can't do that," Caesar told me.

"The hell I can't," I shouted, continuing my rant at the poor nearby fishermen. Relieving stress? No. Instead I was replicating the vehemence of a tirade I'd unleash in response to something like an official calling eight consecutive fouls on Notre Dame.

Caesar was right, however. Our fishing out on the lake did finally have a calming effect, especially after I landed my first bass. By the third day we went out fishing, I was relaxed, at peace, thinking about having landed my dream job and not concerned at all if I landed another fish. Why, I could even wave in friendly fashion to nearby fishermen. I'll have some more to say in a later chapter about the importance of relieving stress and ways to do it.

Notre Dame didn't go in for the huge salaries some schools began to pay their coaches. My base salary rose to only $80,000. But I was getting $150,000 from Reebok, $100,000 to do a TV show, and $50,000 from Champion and Bike. The priests at Notre Dame gave their blessing to these contracts, following the philosophy, "If we don't have to pay him, let him make it in those contracts so that he'll stay here."

Only once was I tempted to leave. I could have had a million-dollar deal over four years with the New York Knicks back in 1980. The deal was that the job was mine once Red Holtzman retired as coach. That was a lot of money back then for any coach, and I would have welcomed the challenge to coach in the pros and the ego trip of being big in New York.

But the kids were reaching high school age, Terry was beginning her successful career at Notre Dame, and Notre Dame was, after all, my dream job. I put ego aside and family first and turned down the opportunity with the Knicks. I have no regrets. It was the right decision.

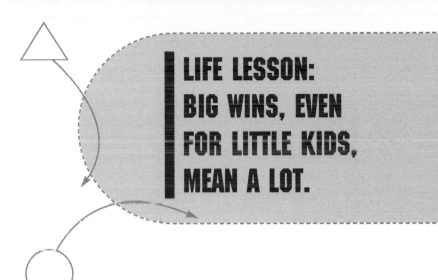

LIFE LESSON: BIG WINS, EVEN FOR LITTLE KIDS, MEAN A LOT.

Chapter 11

Upsetting Experiences

"While Caesar was putting me on about not realizing the significance of beating UCLA, he was serious about what the victory over St. Joachim's meant to him and his young players. You don't have to break a dynasty's eighty-eight-game streak to be elated over a sports victory or some other achievement in life."

Eleven

That first year coaching at Notre Dame was tough. As I noted in an earlier chapter, Austin Carr, greatest scorer in Irish history, had graduated and was gone. Five other seniors also graduated. Injuries further depleted an already thin squad. John Shumate, who had been a star the prior year on the freshman team (freshmen couldn't play on the varsity then), was sidelined with a blood disorder that was life threatening. I had counted on the big center to be a force under the basket, rebounding, scoring, and playing defense, as a sophomore on my first Notre Dame team. He later would be a star, playing a key role in that win two seasons later over UCLA and John Wooden.

But for that first season, 1971–72, we could not compete against the basketball powers, resulting in the routs by Indiana University and UCLA. For the opening game, I had a too-short, all-sophomore lineup. And we had a killer schedule. We finished with six wins and twenty losses.

I'm proud of the players on my first Notre Dame team. Despite that lack of depth and overall talent, they fought as best they could. Six wins was an achievement, not a disgrace. Gary "Goose" Novak, a player from LaSalle, Illinois, saved us from oblivion, averaging what in basketball is called a "double-double": double figures in scoring (nineteen points) and in rebounds (ten). After saving me from an even worse season, Goose went on to something more important, saving patients. He is now a medical doctor.

Goose was still there two seasons later to enjoy that January 19, 1974, upset of UCLA, the team that had run up the score when we had not much of a supporting cast for Goose in my first season. What a wild celebration there was after that exciting 71–70 comeback victory. What a Notre Dame moment!

Amid the after-game celebrating, I called my friend Caesar back in Beacon. "Hey, Caesar, we beat UCLA!" I shouted.

"That's nothing. We beat St. Joachim's!" my friend shouted back.

"Caesar. Hello! We're going to be No. 1 in the country."

"Good, but St. John's hasn't beat St. Joachim's in years."

Caesar coached the St. John's kids in a Catholic Youth Organization league. Indeed, St. Joachim's was then a big and formidable rival.

While Caesar was putting me on about not realizing the significance of beating UCLA, he was serious about what the victory over St. Joachim's meant to him and his young players. You don't have to break a dynasty's eighty-eight-game streak to be elated over a sports victory or some other achievement in life. It's all relative. Caesar was as happy as the imperious, triumphant emperor for whom he was named had been before the Ides of March.

There were to be other Notre Dame moments. In all during my coaching days there, we beat No. 1 teams seven times. I'm not by any means claiming all the credit. You don't win without dedicated players and assistant coaches. But I did have a knack for getting teams ready to play and picking out areas to exploit in facing schools that sometimes had superior material.

Also a key factor in our home-game upsets was the atmosphere, the fan enthusiasm, especially among the students, that we created in the Athletic and Convocation Center—now appropriately named the Edmund P. Joyce Center in honor of Father Joyce. In those days, playing at Notre Dame in front of the cheering, chanting, wildly enthusiastic student body was regarded as one of the toughest away games on any team's schedule. Kind of like playing at Duke these days.

Our second upset of a No. 1 team came on March 5, 1977, when No. 1 San Francisco, led by towering center Bill Cartwright, brought a 29–0 record to the ACC. With our students clapping to the rhythmic chant of "twenty-nine and one, twenty-nine and one," we sent San Francisco home with that record. NBC named the Notre Dame student body as "player of the game." We won 93–82. In the final twelve minutes of the second half, we turned to a "four corners" offense made famous by Coach Dean Smith at North Carolina. I used guard Duck Williams, not normally a scoring leader, in the role of handling the ball in this slow-down offense, and he responded with a twenty-five-point game, seventeen coming as San Francisco was frustrated by the "four corners."

The third upset of a No. 1 team was over the defending national champs, Marquette, on February 26, 1978, at the ACC. My friend Al McGuire had retired as Marquette coach after winning the NCAA championship. But a talented team was back under Coach Hank Raymonds, who had been Al's top assistant. We won 65–59 with a great defensive effort, especially by Bill Hanzlik, as we held Butch Lee, star of the Marquette championship effort, to just fourteen points. A freshman, Kelly Tripucka, who went on to be the best clutch performer I ever coached, took over our offense in the second half, scoring all of his fifteen points in that half and contributing to defense as well.

That team was my Final Four team. We lost in the semifinal game to Duke that year in a thriller. We were down by two points with seconds left but missed a shot that could have tied it and wound up losing 90–86. It's the only time Notre Dame ever made it that far in the tournament. And we just missed the finals.

Our fourth upset of a team with No. 1 standing came on February 27, 1980, at the ACC, where we defeated DePaul, coached by Ray Meyer, who was like a second father to me. Just as a son wants to earn his father's respect, I wanted to win this game, even though I hoped Ray would go on to win every other game on his schedule. Ray had recruited a tremendous team, led by Chicago kids, including leading scorer Mark Aguirre. A great Notre Dame recruiting class, with Tripucka, Tracy Jackson, and Orlando Woolridge, had reached their junior year. We were tied at the end of regulation time. Finally, in the second overtime, I moved those three front-court juniors out from the basket, with the guards in the corners, disrupting DePaul and enabling us finally to prevail 76–74. It also helped that Father Hesburgh said the team Mass earlier that day and was on the bench for the game.

Upset No. 5 of a team ranked No.1 in the nation occurred later that year, on December 27, 1980, as we moved into a new season, with Tripucka, Jackson, and Woolridge in their senior year. This was an especially satisfying win because it came away from home, without a supportive crowd at the ACC. We beat Kentucky at Freedom Hall in Louisville, laughably called a "neutral" site. Because Notre Dame wanted to play the best teams, including Kentucky, and Kentucky wouldn't play at Notre Dame, we ended up meeting year after year in Louisville. While the game wasn't on the Kentucky campus in Lexington, the Louisville crowd was as neutral as Rush Limbaugh on politics. Bourbon flowed freely before the game to fuel the exuberance of many of the Kentucky fans. It was a tough place to play, and my record against Kentucky reflected that. But we won this one, 67–61, with Tripucka taking over the game at crucial times and scoring thirty points.

There have been jokes about Dean Smith being the only one ever able to hold down Michael Jordan's scoring. More than once I was mentioned in similar quips about "holding down" Tripucka's scoring. Kelly sometimes felt that I had. But you need balanced scoring to win consistently. And Kelly, under pressure in a big game, was always there for a scoring burst from the floor or at the foul line.

Our next upset of a No. 1 team also came away from the ACC. On February 22, 1981, at the Rosemont Horizon, we upset No. 1 Virginia, led by Ralph Sampson, a 7-foot, 4-inch giant who was that year the most dominating force in college basketball. Okay, the Rosemont Horizon was in the Chicago area and not exactly a neutral site. We had the crowd on our side. To prepare for Sampson in practice, we actually had a player holding a tennis racket to simulate his size. I used a zone, designed to keep Sampson from beating us and to force other Virginia players to make the shots, if they could. We held Sampson to twenty-two points, a lot of points for most players but half of what he might have scored in a straight-up man-to-man defense. We won 57–56 on a last-second shot from 20 feet out by, of all people, Woolridge, my center, who took the shot from that far out simply because there wasn't time left to pass to anyone else.

That Notre Dame team of 1980–81 was on the losing end of an upset in the NCAA Tournament, when Danny Ainge of Brigham Young University drove through our entire team to hit a last-second winning basket and oust us from the tournament, 51–50. A sad end to the careers of some of the best players ever at Notre Dame—Woolridge, Jackson, and Tripucka. But I've thought that the defeat could have saved us from a worse defeat. If we had won, we would have played Sampson and Virginia again. It might not have been pretty, considering injuries we had suffered and the revenge factor for Virginia. We could not have surprised them a second time with a specially designed zone.

The seventh of our amazing upsets of No. 1 teams came on February 1, 1987, at the ACC, when our unranked kids defeated mighty North Carolina and Dean Smith 60–58 in another come-from-behind thriller. We had no business winning. Our record was not impressive. We lacked the overall talent of past teams. My best player, point guard David Rivers, was just then recovering his full strength after an August traffic accident that nearly took his life. Dean had future pros at every position. North Carolina moved out to a big lead in the first half, and we struggled just to be within nine points with about five minutes left. Rivers then just took over the game, hitting shots and feeding sharp passes to center Gary Voce. Just as before our 1974 upset of UCLA, I sought to build pregame confidence with practice in cutting down the nets. And for the second time, we were able to do what we had practiced, with our game plan and our nets plan.

Except for the fact that new poll standings had not come out yet when we played Missouri on March 3, 1990, at the ACC, we could claim an eighth upset of a No. 1 team. Kansas, which had been No. 1, had lost. Missouri was the logical choice to be the new No. 1 on the day we played them. We clobbered them and their hope for that official No. 1 ranking in the upcoming polls. It got so bad that Missouri coach Norm Stewart benched his starters to give them a wake-up call. Didn't work. We won 98–67.

Chapter 12

Recruiting Promises

"When I'd visit a home in recruiting, I'd try to determine who the hammer was. Who is the one this kid is going to look up to for advice on the final decision of where to go to college? It could be a mother, a father, a grandparent, a favorite aunt, an uncle who had played college ball, a cousin, or the kid's high school coach, who often was there when I visited the family. You had to convince the hammer as well as the youngster."

Twelve

Recruiting is as important as preparing a game plan, or more so, for winning in college basketball. If you can't recruit players with willingness and ability to carry out the game plan in the face of fierce competition, any plan, no matter how brilliant, will fail.

My Beacon upbringing helped me in recruiting top basketball talent for Notre Dame, even though it was known as a football school, not exactly a Duke, North Carolina, or Indiana University in terms of lure for hotshot high school basketball stars. Since I grew up in a diverse community and in a family that was color-blind to racial differences, I was as much at home in a visit to a potential recruit in an African-American neighborhood, where the Fighting Irish weren't the favorite team, as I was in visiting with the Irish Catholic family of another potential recruit.

Strange as it may sound, being an undertaker's son also helped in recruiting. When I was in high school, my father often took me with him to the home where relatives of the deceased made final arrangements for the wake and funeral. Though sad, they still had to make decisions on the right way to send their loved one off to eternity. They wanted the right suit and tie or dress. The right casket. The right wake. The right service. The right people notified. The right wording of the obituary in the newspaper.

There was always a person we identified as "the hammer." That was the person who took the initiative, no matter the grief, to make the final decisions or at least to influence and guide the others to those decisions. It could be a spouse, a daughter, a son, or, if the deceased was younger, a father or mother or grand-parent. Identifying this central figure that could and would take charge at this time of stress and sorrow was important in getting arrangements set.

When I'd visit a home in recruiting, I'd try to determine who the hammer was. Who is the one this kid is going to look up to for advice on the final decision of where to go to college? It could be a mother, a father, a grandparent, a favorite aunt, an uncle who had played college ball, a cousin, or the kid's high school coach, who often was there when I visited the family. You had to convince the hammer as well as the youngster.

My father would visit a family to talk about a death. I'd visit to talk about life ahead in college. Sensitivities were involved in both situations as a family considered what would be right for a loved one. I'd emphasize Notre Dame academics. The only guar-antee was that we intended for the boy to get a degree in four years. He would take courses leading to a degree, not basket-weaving and history-of-the-fast-break classes to get by until completing basketball eligibility. He would not leave with useless credits, no diploma, and no actual college education.

Mike DeCicco, the Notre Dame fencing coach, was asked by Father Joyce to establish an academic advisor office for athletes. Mike took the new additional duties as seriously as he did his coaching. And his coaching led to five national fencing championships. Mike kept track of whether the players were attending class and how they were doing. If they needed tutoring help in a tough class, they got it. If they cut classes, they got something else. We suggested that Mike would take an épée to the hide of a player who skipped a class. He never did. But the players knew he was strict in his demands for attendance and grades. They also knew I'd back him up with a suspension for class cutting.

If DeCicco stopped by during a practice to see one of the players, I'd send the player off with him forthwith. Sometimes at the start of a practice, I'd say, "DeCicco needs to see one of you guys." I'd pause; maybe even go on with some other item, acting as though I'd been distracted. They'd all squirm before I got back to naming the player who was to report to DeCicco to clear up some problem. Problems indeed were cleared up, as shown by the 100 percent graduation record for my players.

Since I didn't embarrass a kid who was benched for a class cut by announcing it to the news media, our fans didn't always understand why a player wasn't in the game. Once I sat a starting player for cutting a class. As the game went on, the student section started calling for the popular player. They were chanting his name. The call got louder as we went through the second half. Finally, I called the player from his seat at the end of the bench. Excited, he came over, ready to go in the game. "Hey," I suggested, "why don't you go up to the student section to find out what they want?" He did not go in the game.

Two of my best players, Adrian Dantley and Gary Brokaw—both on my personal "first team" of players I coached at Notre Dame—turned pro before their senior years. Both promised me that they would return to get their degrees. They did. Each was very proud of the achievement, and so was I.

Most high school basketball stars fully expect someday to play in the National Basketball Association. An average of about one a year of my players at Notre Dame did achieve that level. Two were stars with teams winning multiple championships: John Paxson, one of Michael Jordan's favorite teammates on the Chicago Bulls, and Bill Laimbeer, favorite of no opposing team in the NBA as he elbowed to rebound records with the Detroit Pistons.

Odds of making it in the NBA are slim for even some excellent college players. You may be an outstanding 6-foot-7 college forward, but the pros may well select someone 6-10 who is just as good. High school stars entering college assume they are indestructible, but a blown-out knee can end NBA hopes and a college career as well. Maybe the potential recruit didn't pay much attention when I stressed that a Notre Dame degree always would be there for life after basketball, whether a career extended into the pros or was cut short by injury. However, the hammer, older and usually more realistic, often understood.

The Notre Dame network, with Notre Dame alumni clubs everywhere, can help a graduate. And even beyond alumni ranks, there is respect for that diploma and for what is learned in the Notre Dame experience. Mike Mitchell is a good example. Mike is the only player to whom I ever gave a game ball in my two decades of coaching at Notre Dame. He was one of the best high school players in California, and he no doubt assumed, as high school stars of his ability do, that he would play pro at the NBA level. After showing such promise during his freshman season at Notre Dame, knee problems developed in his sophomore year. There was surgery. Then further injury prior to his junior year. Doctors advised him to bypass his senior year of basketball. But he was determined to play. Because of his drive and the inspiration he provided, I named Mike captain for his senior year, the 1981–82 season. Play he did, though clearly not up to his prior potential.

I've noted my successful strategy in picking an opposing player as our sixth man, almost inviting that opponent to shoot, while doubling up elsewhere on defense. That strategy also was used at times against us, as it was on February 7, 1982, when we played San Francisco, then ranked No. 7 in the nation. They were determined that we would not upset them again as we had in 1977, when they were ranked No. 1. They doubled up on Paxson, sloughing off on Mike Mitchell, my gimpy guard with the lowest scoring average among the starters. They wanted Mike, not Paxson, to take shots. In the best game of his career, Mike hit six of seven shots in the first half as we took a lead and made seven of eight free throws in the second half as they changed strategy to press him. We upset the Dons again. Mike couldn't play in the NBA. But he had his Notre Dame degree and went on to become president of the sales division of Nestle U.S.A.

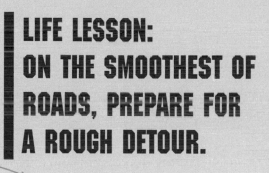

Chapter 13

Always Have a Backup

"In 1991, Rev. Edward 'Monk' Malloy, university president; Rev. William Beauchamp, executive vice president; and Richard Rosenthal, the athletic director, made clear they wanted my resignation. They wanted me to resign (or be fired) so that the basketball program could head in a different direction. On April 15, 1991, I resigned. And the basketball program headed in a different direction, not to return to the NCAA Tournament for a decade.

My backup? Before I went to the news conference to announce my resignation, I placed a call to the President of the United States. George H. W. Bush took my call, as I knew he would, with White House operators contacting him in Alabama.

'Mr. President, I want you to know first, before my news conference today, that I'm resigning as basketball coach of Notre Dame,' I said. 'And I'm ready to come to work for you.'

'When do you want to start?' was the presidential response. My reply: "When is the next plane to Washington?"

Thirteen

In the locker room when I coached at Notre Dame, I posted a sign with this message: "To Be Successful: 1. Listen. 2. Talk to each other. 3. Concentrate on each situation." Another admonition I taught to players, assistant coaches, student managers, trainers, and secretaries was, "Don't assume. Follow up. Always have a backup." This, I stressed, was not just about success in basketball but in dealing with challenges throughout life.

Winter travel from South Bend to away basketball games provided many an example of the need for a backup plan. If we had a scheduled flight from South Bend to New York, with a stop in Cincinnati, I insisted on a backup schedule. What if heavy snow in South Bend or Cincinnati cancelled that portion of the flight? We always had alternative travel plans.

"Always have a backup." I did when it became apparent that new administrators at Notre Dame wanted a new basketball coach, their own coach, not the one hired by Father Hesburgh and Father Joyce, both of whom had retired. So, despite twenty years of success, 393 wins, a 67 percent winning percentage, fourteen teams advancing to the NCAA Tournament, including six in the last seven years and a 100 percent graduation rate of the fifty-six players who completed four years during my time as coach, it was time to go.

These things happen. It happened to my friend Bob Knight, despite his outstanding record at Indiana University. Administrators who hadn't hired him found a way to fire him when they wanted a change. In football at Notre Dame, an incoming president triggered the sudden firing of Coach Tyrone Willingham.

In 1991 Rev. Edward "Monk" Malloy, university president; Rev. William Beauchamp, executive vice president; and Richard Rosenthal, the athletic director, made clear they wanted my resignation. They wanted me to resign (or be fired) so that the basketball program could head in a different direction. On April 15, 1991, I resigned. And the basketball program headed in a different direction, not to return to the NCAA Tournament for a decade.

My backup? Before I went to the news conference to announce my resignation, I placed a call to the president of the United States. George H. W. Bush took my call, as I knew he would, with White House operators contacting him in Alabama.

"Mr. President, I want you to know first, before my news conference today, that I'm resigning as basketball coach of Notre Dame," I said. "And I'm ready to come to work for you."

"When do you want to start?" was the presidential response. My reply: "When is the next plane to Washington?"

Well, Washington bureaucracy takes a little longer than that. Deciding on the right job took longer in my case because of fear by one Cabinet member that I might challenge him in the future for a presidential nomination and due to my own concern about finding a post in which I could provide valuable service to the president and to the nation. I wasn't just looking for salary. Not when higher salaries beckoned in television or coaching. Nor was I looking for some fancy title that didn't involve much work. I wanted to work, as hard and with as much enthusiasm as in my coaching, and to focus now on national goals, not just on a goal of higher ranking in the basketball polls.

An ironic aspect of this is that I had not planned to coach much longer anyway. I had decided long ago in a philosophy that began developing back in Beacon at my dad's funeral home that I wanted time in life to try new things, see new places, and develop new interests rather than coach into old age. I was ready for new challenges, and what could be more challenging than working for your president, your country.

I knew the president would take my call that day because he was and is a friend. Sure, he then was "Mr. President," and that of course was the title of respect with which I addressed him. But I had known him as "George," a friend who had been a guest at my cabin on Lake Michigan. Two decades before, I had met Bush at a charity golf tournament in Dayton, Ohio. Ara Parseghian, the great Notre Dame football coach who did so much to help me become a part of Notre Dame and to introduce me to influential people at the national level, brought me to the tournament. I met important people from Washington, Hollywood, the auto industry, the oil industry, and other businesses, as well as from college and professional sports. Bush was then an ambassador.

We became friends. It continued through his years as vice president. During the 1988 campaign, when Vice President Bush was running for president, he spoke at Notre Dame on November 1, just a week before the election. His Democratic opponent, Michael Dukakis, had been invited also but had declined.

While I was a Democrat—and still am—I had joined the ranks of "Reagan Democrats," supporting Ronald Reagan. Naturally, I was supporting Bush. I knew and respected him as an outstanding individual and a good friend, and I agreed with his commitment to the peace-through-strength concepts of the Reagan administration. Bush was pledging not just strength but willingness to meet with Soviet leader Mikhail Gorbachev "at the earliest time that would serve the interests of world peace."

In his Notre Dame speech, Bush differentiated his philosophy from that of his Democratic opponent in a way that brought to mind my disagreements with some of the Democrats on the national level. He said, "And it seems to me, after six months of a hard-fought campaign, that what it all comes down to is this: One of us represents the American mainstream—and one of us does not. One of us holds mainstream views and stands for mainstream values—and one of us does not. And 'mainstream' isn't just the middle—it's the big full-hearted center, it's the traditions and the faith and the beliefs that have guided this country for two hundred years."

The mostly student crowd that packed Notre Dame's Stepan Center gave an enthusiastic response to Bush's speech. So did I. Riding with him in his limo during his visit to Notre Dame, I told him, "You're going to win. And I want to come to work for you."

"You'll still be coaching," he laughed. He thought I was joking.

No, even then, in 1988, I knew problems were looming with the troika of Malloy, Rosenthal, and Beauchamp and that it was going to get ugly. It did. And I had a backup. Finding the right job in a Bush administration already staffed and more than halfway through the president's term took longer than I anticipated, in large measure due to my own insistence on finding the right job, not just *a* job. The right job finally was found: running Operation Weed and Seed, a program through which we were starting to win the battle to reclaim neighborhoods from drug dealers, gangs, and violence.

First, however, the president and Vice President Dan Quayle had lined up a possible post in the Department of Education. Quayle also was a friend. I had known him since he was a senator from Indiana. In fact, some influential Democrats in Indiana, including the late Sen. R. Vance Hartke, had sought to persuade me to run against Quayle in his bid for reelection to a second term in the Senate. While I joked about getting Knight as my campaign manager and listened politely to promises of support, I had no intention of running against Quayle or seeking any elective office at that time.

After talking with Education Secretary Lamar Alexander at a state dinner at the White House, my interest in a post in the Department of Education waned. He was cold, showing no enthusiasm for my joining his staff. Then I met with Alexander's senior staff. Again, I found no enthusiasm, no vision, no incentive to join their bureaucracy.

Alexander, a former governor of Tennessee who was known for walking across his state and wearing plaid shirts as campaign gimmicks, had the White House as his personal goal. He was to run for the Republican presidential nomination in 1996, losing to

Bob Dole, and to announce for the presidency again in 2000, dropping out early as George W. Bush became the clear front-runner. Alexander's own presidential ambitions kept him from any welcome for me as a member of his department. He apparently felt threatened by me, believing that I might, if successful in the administration, seek the presidential nomination. Well, I did think about it. But then I just wanted a job in which I could be of service to the president, with the future to take care of itself.

"I don't like this," I told Quayle of my reception in the Department of Education. "I don't think they have the vision." They did have, I suppose, a vision of a President Alexander.

Finally, Quayle and Bush, who met for lunch every Thursday, decided that my familiarity with basketball recruiting in all the big cities of the nation, and many small ones as well, would make me the person they were looking for to head Operation Weed and Seed, an innovative effort that required going into troubled areas of cities to launch a coordinated effort to weed out the drug dealers and gangs and seed those areas with programs to provide economic hope and positive choices for kids.

The program was part of the war on drugs. I interviewed with Bob Martinez, the drug czar, and we were in agreement on the value of the program. We shared a vision of what could be accomplished. To achieve it, however, I knew that I needed a staff that was my own. Just as I needed a loyal secretary and loyal assistant coaches at Notre Dame, I needed similar help to launch the weeding and seeding. So I requested a secretary and two assistants. By this time the Bush administration was in its final year. I went to London, where Terry was running the Notre Dame law program that semester, and awaited word from the White House. The call came in February. Done deal. I get whatever I want for staff. The job's mine. The president wants me to take it.

Since I was signed up to do commentary on CBS for "March Madness," the NCAA Basketball Tournament, we decided that I might as well go ahead with that, building more name recognition for when the announcement of my appointment came. As Duke was heading to the NCAA championship, I was so anxious to get started with Weed and Seed that I headed to Trenton, New Jersey, the pilot city for the program, to see what was happening. It was off to a great start. I was enthused, confident that this program would help our cities and help the president achieve a reputation for a successful "Domestic Storm" to complement his "Desert Storm" triumph.

"You really believe in this program, don't you?" the president said, delighted, when I told him of my observations. Yes, I did and still do, if only it could be implemented now as we had envisioned it then.

Chapter 14

Weeding and Seeding

"If a young executive, one of the 'haves,' develops an addiction, he can go to the human resources director at the corporation and seek help for his problem with cocaine or heroin. Well, with praise for coming forward to seek help, the executive is off to the Betty Ford Clinic or some other treatment center, with the cost paid by the corporation. Then, after completion of treatment, the conquering hero is welcomed back to the job, maybe with ice cream and cake for the office celebration on the day of the triumphant return. No penalty for all the illegal purchases he made.

On the other side of the economic divide, a 'have-not' who gets hooked—like the women I met at a Philadelphia homeless center for crack-addicted mothers—has no human resources director to go to for help, no chance of treatment at the Betty Ford Clinic, and no ice cream and cake for even the most valiant effort to break the habit. Since some of those women turned to prostitution in desperation for money, they faced penalties of jail. They also faced risk of death through overdose or violence."

Fourteen

During a Rose Garden ceremony honoring the U.S. Winter Olympic team on April 8, 1992, President Bush announced my appointment to a newly created post as a top assistant in the White House Office of National Drug Control Policy, with responsibility for an expanded Operation Weed and Seed.

A United Press International story reported that "Phelps has no prior experience in anti-narcotics efforts and it was not immediately clear why he was chosen for the post." A spokesman for the Justice Department was quoted: "A guy like Phelps is certainly the kind of individual that can attract and coordinate the kinds of groups that we anticipate are going to want to be part of this."

The "kinds of groups" we needed as part of the program in blighted neighborhoods already were familiar to me. From recruiting in poor neighborhoods and in drug-infested, gang-infiltrated high schools in a quest for good athletes who also were good kids, I knew there were people who deplored the conditions and would work together, if given the opportunity, to drive out the dealers, to improve conditions, to save the kids.

Not only did the president appoint me to a challenging job, he gave me freedom to meet the challenge. In his introduction he made it clear that I would be working "alongside" Martinez, the drug czar, and Attorney General Bill Barr, who was responsible for the law enforcement and prosecution efforts in the weeding. "Alongside." That meant that I reported, just as they did, to the president. I didn't have to report to Martinez or Barr. This drove Barr nuts. If there was a disagreement, I went to Quayle or Bush, and they helped me to slash through the bureaucracy to get things done.

Just the knowledge that I had the president's ear was a help in getting a prompt, positive response, not excuses and delays. One example was when I found we had no Hispanic community police officers in Hispanic neighborhoods in a project.

"How come we don't have Hispanics?"

The response: "They can't pass the tests."

"Then change the tests," I said. There are bright, qualified Hispanics for almost any job. If none could pass the test to be a cop, it seemed to me that the test was in some way unfair. In our community-policing concept we needed cops whom the people in the neighborhoods would trust. These officers were to get out of squad cars, walk the streets as the old-time beat officers did, or ride bicycles, developing a closer contact and better relationship with the neighborhood. But get officers who understand the language and the people of the neighborhood. Or forget about community policing. I got results rather than bureaucratic excuses.

I sometimes drove bureaucrats wacky. Also, I drove them to get things done. We had successes in the twenty cities around the country where we weeded and seeded, often finding surprising allies—even gang members—in lessening violence, restoring hope, and encouraging people to learn skills for useful jobs.

Since I had been preparing for and anxious to start this new chapter of my life, I hit the ground weeding and seeding. Weeding? We marshaled the forces of local, state, and federal law-enforcement agencies to arrest or at least clear the streets of the pushers and punks who made life unsafe for folks who wanted to live their lives without fear. Without fear of their children being solicited to try or peddle drugs. Without fear of bullets shattering their windows and their lives as gangs battled over drug turf. Seeding? We promoted programs to keep schools open after classes were dismissed for the day. Right after school is the danger time for kids who hit the streets with nowhere to go, no parent at home, no wholesome activity in which to participate.

Too often too many of these kids engage in unsafe sex, resulting in children having children. Or they get involved with drugs, looking up to the pushers, who seem to have the only well-paying jobs in the neighborhood. Or they join gangs, frequently for protection from rival gangs on the streets, winding up shooting someone or being shot.

In cities I visited, we obtained positive news coverage for our efforts, thanks in part to my name recognition from basketball. A story in the *Post-Standard* in Syracuse, New York, was typical of the coverage. It told of my plea at the New York State School Boards Association conference on school sports. My effort was to back after-school activities and resist cuts in high school sports and other extracurricular activities.

Staff writer David Ramsey wrote that I "employed the emotion and idealism of a preacher" and added: "Last time Phelps visited Syracuse—in 1990, his next-to-last season at Notre Dame—he led the Fighting Irish to a 66–65 last-second victory over Syracuse University. As the game ended, he leaped and skipped and danced on the Carrier Dome floor while 32,747 fans and a national television audience watched." On this visit, Ramsey wrote, I was beseeching, not celebrating.

True. This game had not been won. We were in the middle of a struggle for the children of the nation. We knew that we had to do something first in every targeted area about drugs and violence. The two problems are related. And they involve a double standard. The "haves" buy drugs with little risk and, if hooked, get treatment. The "have-nots" kill each other in turf wars over the sales and, if hooked, get prison.

In New York, Washington, Chicago, and other urban areas, people with money were driving in from the suburbs to buy illegal drugs from the sellers in the poorest, violence-prone neighborhoods of the city. On a Friday or Saturday night, suburbanites with money would drive in droves over the George Washington Bridge in New York City, go to the neighborhoods where drugs were sold on the streets, get their stuff, and go back home with no risk. Gangs controlling drug sales aren't going to shoot their customers. They don't want to hurt business. They only shot rival gang members in battles over control of turf and over the big bucks coming from the sales.

If a young executive, one of the "haves," develops an addiction, he can go to the human resources director at the corporation and seek help for his problem with cocaine or heroin. Well, with praise for coming forward to seek help, the executive is off to the Betty Ford Clinic or some other treatment center, with the cost paid by the corporation. Then, after completion of treatment, the conquering hero is welcomed back to the job, maybe with ice cream and cake for the office celebration on the day of the triumphant return. No penalty for all the illegal purchases he made.

On the other side of the economic divide, a "have-not" who gets hooked—like the women I met at a Philadelphia homeless center for crack-addicted mothers—has no human resources director to go to for help, no chance of treatment at the Betty Ford Clinic, and no ice cream and cake for even the most valiant effort to break the habit. Since some of those women turned to prostitution in desperation for money, they faced penalties of jail. They also faced risk of death through overdose or violence.

Police ranks were too thin to do much in some of the most troubled areas other than to seek arrest of gang members after they had murdered rivals. That's why we marshaled law enforcement from all levels for the weeding in those areas. At that center in Philadelphia for those crack-addicted mothers, I met at one point with ten of the most unfortunate "have-nots" of society. They told of such horrors as living in crack houses, having crack babies, suffering terrible abuse, being raped, and turning to the most shameful of things to get money for an overpowering habit.

One woman told of having once had $12,000 in public assistance and a $4,000 part-time job, enough to scrape by. But she was caught making too much money beyond the cap at that time and lost her welfare. She turned to crack. It took control of her. And she became a prostitute to pay for her crack habit.

Some of the women finally were getting treatment and hope. I often wonder what happened to them. How many survived?

How many went back to addiction and died from drugs or through violence? How many took advantage of a new start to get a better education and jobs and to be good mothers? How many of their children are successful? How many children followed along the same path to addiction?

A few of these women offered ideas for how to weed out the horrors of the crack world and how to help in freeing the addicted. Did they believe that I really cared and wanted to help? I don't know. But I think some of them did.

We tried to convince people in the targeted neighborhoods that it was possible with their help to end the self-destructive life of drugs and violence. We tried. They tried. The nation still has not committed, however, to the type of all-out effort needed. It's sad that this plague of drugs and violence still afflicts the nation today. Most of the people in those neighborhoods were tired of the shootings, the drug dealing, and the vice. They welcomed formation of neighborhood-watch groups that would report illegal activities. Where community police and neighborhood-watch groups became a team, they did indeed drive out the bad elements. They still can. More communities should turn to this approach.

One way to curb gang violence was to go to the gangs. That I did. So did Jim Brown, the great running back who played in college for Syracuse and then in the National Football League for the Cleveland Browns. A strong argument can be made that Jim was the greatest running back ever, compiling a 5.2-yards-per-carry average in the NFL, winning the rushing title in eight of the nine seasons he played and scoring 126 touchdowns while never missing a game.

Jim retired from football at the top of his game after the 1965 season. More achievements were ahead in a movie career, with roles in more than thirty films, including *The Dirty Dozen* and *Ice Station Zebra*, and in seeking to curb gang violence and turn around the lives of troubled inner-city kids.

I went to Jim's house in the hills above Los Angeles in September of 1992 to talk with him about our efforts and to learn from his approach with Amer-I-Can, the program he founded in

1988 to promote self-esteem and the desire and determination for success among folks in impoverished communities. He fully understood the concept of Weed and Seed, including the need to do something first about gang violence.

At his home to meet with us were members of the Bloods and the Crips, rival Los Angeles gangs that had been at war, killing each other in violence that made neighborhoods unsafe for everyone. Among the gang members, I spotted a tall young man who looked familiar. I asked, "Are you . . . ?" He was indeed. He was a former UCLA player.

Mistakenly, many assume that gang members are young men with no potential. Sometimes they have potential, even the opportunity to use it, but for one reason or another they fail to use that potential, that opportunity. Mistakenly, many assume that gang members lack intelligence. Intelligence is needed just to survive on the streets and to reach a leadership position.

Jim knew that. He sought to appeal to the potential and intelligence of some of those gang members to convince them to stop the killing. And he was successful in negotiating a cease-fire between the Bloods and the Crips, an "impossibility" that was made possible.

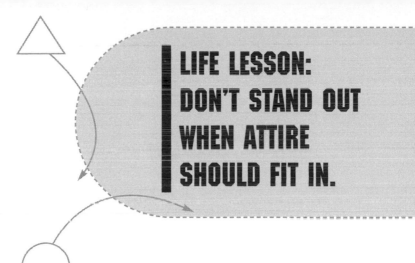

**LIFE LESSON:
DON'T STAND OUT
WHEN ATTIRE
SHOULD FIT IN.**

Chapter 15

Washington Sightseeing: Where Tourists Fear to Tread

"One incident when I was with Orlando and J. J. showed an unfortunate stereotyping. After a tour through one of the Washington neighborhoods, we were running to catch a bus. J. J. reached the street and was trying to flag down the bus. Orlando and I were running through a park to catch up, Orlando in front of me. A gentleman sitting on a bench saw me running after a young African-American and called out: 'Good afternoon, officer.'"

Fifteen

In a Washington neighborhood troubled by gang violence, I arranged a meeting that turned out to be an emotional experience. Lots of crying. Lots of anger. Lots of progress. Jim Brown, with the commanding presence of a superstar, came to challenge the audience to seek the self-esteem offered through his Amer-I-Can principles. He would speak last.

Also invited to participate were

— A group of mothers whose sons and daughters had been gunned down on the streets, sometimes as targets in gang battles over territory or drugs, sometimes as innocent victims who were at the wrong place when bullets flew. When I was in Washington on Thursday nights, I went to the support-group meetings of these women. I knew of the pain they felt and of the anguish and bitterness they would express. They wanted the violence to stop.

— A neighborhood-watch group for that area known as the Wise Up Coalition. Members of the coalition were there to explain how it was possible to keep an eye on the danger spots and perhaps jot down some license-plate numbers that could be of use to police in making the area safer. They had come to view police as possible partners rather than feared enemies.

— Two streetwise young African-Americans, Orlando and J. J., who knew what was going on and had themselves been involved in some destructive behavior. They would explain the mind-set of the gangs and what was required just to survive on the streets. They were to be of enormous help to me, serving as protectors and guides in taking me to the downside sites in our nation's capital.

The meeting took place in an old, vacated storefront that had been converted into a church. The place was packed, over a hundred people there. Orlando and J. J. spoke first. They were blunt in telling the tale of the streets, explaining what it was like and why there was violence.

These young men were tough to sell on what I was attempting. Before they would confide, I had to win their respect. Sure, being known as a basketball coach helped. There was respect for that, in part because a basketball career was looked upon as a way to escape from the ghetto. Also, my lifetime association with blacks, from childhood in Beacon to the days of successfully recruiting outstanding black players for Notre Dame, was an advantage in mutual understanding.

Initially, they challenged whether I really cared or wanted to help: "You're just another white honky, Digger, and we don't trust you." One challenge, which may seem strange coming from the violent streets, was to read a book. They told me to read *The Autobiography of Malcolm X: As Told to Alex Haley*. I did. It helped me understand the mind-set, and as I read of his philosophy, I was enlightened to the fact that Malcolm X was not advocating violence. This is a book I was later to recommend to Vice President Dan Quayle, who read it, understood the message, and was to quote from it in his plea for better racial understanding.

When the mothers of the slain children spoke, there were tears and an understandable lashing out at the terrible conditions and violence. Orlando, sitting in the back of the room after his presentation, abruptly stood up, loudly interrupting one of the mothers with some rude street language. "Shut up!" I yelled.

"These women listened to your presentation. Give them respect." He sat down. Just as sometimes with coaching, it was necessary to make a point quickly and firmly.

As the meeting went on, tension lessened, understanding grew, and focus shifted from the horrid past to a possible better future. Brown was magnificent in a closing presentation. And at the emotional conclusion, there were Orlando and J. J. and the mothers hugging.

Orlando and J. J. took me places where I would not have dared to venture alone and enabled contact with people who other-wise would not have opened up to me or listened to me. My view was that selling Operation Weed and Seed in neighborhoods was just like any sales effort: You've got to know the territory.

One incident when I was with Orlando and J. J. showed an unfortunate stereotyping. After a tour through one of the Washington neighborhoods, we were running to catch a bus. J. J. reached the street and was trying to flag down the bus. Orlando and I were running through a park to catch up, Orlando in front of me. A gentleman sitting on a bench saw me running after a young African-American and called out, "Good afternoon, officer."

At one meeting in Chicago in a neighborhood just east of what was then Comiskey Park, I was accompanied by FBI agent Peter Buckley. Jim Brown had arranged for an influential contact to organize the meeting. It was valuable and lengthy. And it was dark when we got back to a parking garage downtown at the Federal Building, where I had parked my rental car. We couldn't find the car. Agent Buckley was very concerned. Heck, I figured I'd simply catch a cab. "Peter, don't worry about it," I told him. "It's just a rental car."

"Digger, I have to worry about anything you do," Buckley told me. "I've got orders." He said FBI Deputy Director Larry Potts had admonished, "No matter where he goes, make sure nothing happens to Digger."

My personal safety really had not been a concern to me. We established trust in the neighborhoods I visited. People like J. J. and Orlando paved the way. So did Jim Brown and people involved in his program. Nothing was going to happen. But I understood the concern at FBI headquarters. Wouldn't have looked good if the Weed and Seed guy from the White House was gunned down in some meeting with gang members. Also, I appreciated their concern.

There was no need for concern about danger in the parking garage. We found the car. We had been looking for the color of the car as it was seen in daylight. Lights at night in the garage distorted the color. Car found. No plot.

When the FBI was with me, we sometimes traveled in a car that had been obtained through drug-case forfeitures. One agent in Los Angeles would take me to certain areas in a Spyder sports car. That was okay. It could engender some respect. Wisely, however, the agents rejected using a robin's-egg-blue convertible Rolls Royce for an inner-city trip in Los Angeles.

Image was important in the neighborhoods. It was better to wear jeans and a sweatshirt for a tour of a troubled area. For a meeting with community leaders, of course, it was a suit and tie. The accompanying FBI agent packed a gun on an ankle if it was a suit affair, on the stomach under the sweatshirt if it was an event calling for informal attire.

We didn't have a lot of funding for Weed and Seed. So, at a meeting at the Justice Department with U.S. attorneys from around the nation, I urged that they seek ways to utilize community assets already in place to help in promoting the economic empowerment so vital in keeping weeds from growing anew. The U.S. attorney in New Orleans, a city for which I have a special affection, especially now as it fights back after suffering so much from Hurricane Katrina, came up with a great concept for seeding.

Economic empowerment was vital then, even before Katrina, in neighborhoods such as the now-devastated Ninth Ward. Much of the population did not share in the prosperity from tourism and the bonanza of Mardi Gras. Unemployment was high. Poverty was rampant. Inner-city neighborhoods were beset by the problems of gangs, drugs, violence, and children having children.

Tourists ate fine cuisine and drank expensive wines at Antoine's and enjoyed breakfast at Brennan's. Corporate executives and their clients cheered for the National Football League New Orleans Saints in choice seats in the Superdome.

Folks from the sprawling-poverty part of New Orleans couldn't afford to walk in the front doors of the famous restaurants or enter a Superdome gate—unless they washed dishes at the restaurants or swept up at the Dome after an NFL game.

Even with unemployment, there were job openings, opportunities. The trouble was that many of the unemployed either lacked the skills needed to fill openings or had no idea how to market skills and abilities that could enable them to escape poverty.

The New Orleans concept involved going into the public-housing units to find women who were good cooks. Unemployed, single moms there weren't likely to prepare for the kids a dinner of something like "le filet de pompano en papillote," a specialty at Antoine's. But they might dish out a mean gumbo. They might do wonders with red beans and rice. They might, despite poverty, spice up and spruce up low-cost food in Cajun style to taste good and look good.

The second step was to get a professional chef or the owner of a restaurant to do some mentoring, to help these women adapt their skills to fill a real need in catering. New Orleans was then—and is becoming again—a city of myriad events for which food is catered, such as luncheon meetings, convention activities, evening receptions, and night parties.

These women already knew how to cook the Cajun food that was popular for such events. Why couldn't they learn, with proper mentoring, to cook in the required volume and to land contracts for their catering business? They could. This was economic empowerment. It is a concept that could work in many areas, matching skills with needs in unique ways to fight unemployment and poverty.

I annoyed them in Washington with my insistence on making unannounced visits. Attorney General Bill Barr wanted his Justice Department people alerted well in advance for their planning purposes. But I wanted to see reality, not how everything was spruced up for an official visit, not how everything was arranged nice and pretty for photo opportunities for the news media. Once, when I was traveling with Vice President Quayle for an announced visit, I noticed that the pretty green grass at the visit site was fresh turf just planted. I didn't want to see a targeted neighborhood after a fresh coat of paint was slapped on to cover continued deterioration.

We were making progress. Weed and Seed was working. Bill Clinton seemed to think so, too. On the night after that Chicago meeting, I stopped at a Chicago Bears football game. Clinton, then the Democratic nominee for president, was there that September night as a guest of Chicago Mayor Richard M. Daley. Earlier, I had briefed the mayor on Weed and Seed. When we met while leaving the game, the mayor and I told Clinton why I was in Chicago and of my efforts with Weed and Seed.

"I really like this program," Clinton told me.

After Clinton won the election, his transition people did show interest in continuation of the program, but it was downsized. It lost momentum. My dream had been for a national program, not just continuation of the effort on a small scale in a few cities.

On January 19, 1993, the day before the presidential inauguration, Orlando and J. J. came to my office. "It's over," I told them sadly. It was. For them. For me. For our concepts and dreams of a successful program to take on our nation's biggest domestic problems of drugs, violence, and poverty.

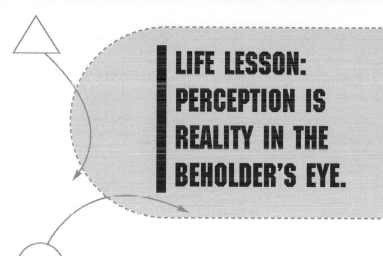

Chapter 16

Dan Quayle's Hot Potato(e)

"But Dan Quayle is neither dumb nor a joke. He took seriously the vice-presidential responsibilities of being informed on national and international issues with which he would have been confronted if suddenly thrust into the presidency. Faithfully and well, he carried out many important assignments from President Bush."

Sixteen

I was with Dan Quayle on the day during the 1992 campaign when he was stung by a spelling bee. The vice president had come to Trenton, New Jersey, on June 15, following a speech in New York earlier that day, to join me for what was to have been an opportunity for us to show the nation, through news-media coverage, what was being accomplished by Operation Weed and Seed. Instead, the news media were to report not on a weed or a seed but on a potato(e).

Dan's alleged misspelling of "potato" enhanced—cemented for many Americans—an unfair image of him as dumb, a joke, a human gaffe machine. I say "alleged misspelling" because Quayle wasn't the one who added the "e." If Dan had not been stymied by an image that was unfortunate and unfair, could he have gone on to serve as a great president? I'm not claiming that he would have been a great president or even a good one. We'll never know. We don't know for sure in advance about whether any president will achieve greatness or fall far short.

But Dan Quayle is neither dumb nor a joke. He took seriously the vice-presidential responsibilities of being informed on national and international issues with which he would have been confronted if suddenly thrust into the presidency. Faithfully and well, he carried out many important assignments from President Bush.

Still, he could not shake a lightweight image that began to form the moment he first was introduced to the American people as George Bush's choice as a running mate. Last-minute notification that he was the choice for vice-presidential nominee necessitated rushing, with no remarks prepared, to the announcement of his selection at the 1988 Republican National Convention in New Orleans. He had to push through the crowd at a plaza to reach the platform at which Bush, the presidential nominee, would name his running mate. Dan appeared to be out of breath, excited, and unsure of what to say. Well, he was. It was kind of like tripping on the front porch as he came to say "hi" to the American people.

A few other unfortunate mistakes—and he did make mistakes in moving from senator from Indiana to vice president—resulted in the news media watching for any flub, every stumble. A gaffe by Quayle that might have been ignored or not even noticed if committed by other public figures was news.

Worse, it then provided material for Leno and Letterman on their late-night shows. No conspiracy. It's just a fact that when an image begins to stick, rightly or wrongly, actions that enhance that image become more significant. Bob Knight briefly reprimanding a student who had seemed disrespectful would never have made headlines or ended his Indiana University coaching career if Bob's image as a coach with a chair-throwing temper had not been perpetuated and, finally, exaggerated.

I met Quayle at the airport in Trenton. The motorcade headed for Luis Munoz-Rivera School, also known as Junior High No. 5, an elementary-junior high that had been built as a school for black students before the 1946 school integration in Trenton. It was a school we played in basketball back when I coached at Junior High No. 4.

We would show the vice president the after-school programs aimed at getting kids off the troubled streets in a poverty area and into constructive activities. Through the news media, we thought, we also would show it off for the nation, helping to promote Weed and Seed to other communities as well. As the motorcade approached the school, Dan noticed that women in the neighborhood, mostly African-Americans, had come out on their porches, a lot of them holding babies. He wanted to halt the motorcade to talk with them. How were they surviving? What did they need? What would help? What wouldn't? Those were questions that concerned him because of his determination to understand the lives and problems of minorities, particularly those in poverty, with whom he had little contact in his privileged upbringing and education.

"We can't stop," I insisted. "We have to get to the school. The kids are waiting. We've got all those after-school programs they want you to see." But I knew he was going to insist on stopping to talk with those women on the way back to the airport.

Dan was sincere in his quest for better understanding. Since he was aware of how I was accepted and felt at ease in the most troubled African-American areas, he would talk to me about racial understanding. That was a part of my upbringing in Beacon, growing up in a family that was color-blind. My understanding of troubled areas grew as a coach recruiting at times in some bad areas. Bad areas didn't mean all the kids were bad.

Once on a flight on *Air Force Two*, I urged Dan to read *The Autobiography of Malcolm X*. Malcolm was not advocating violence. Dan not only read the book; he soon was quoting from it.

First of all at the school, we saw a drill team do its stuff in the gym. Then we went to a classroom for a self-esteem program for kids who really needed the encouragement. Dan paid proper attention, but his mind was on something else. "Let's go outside," Dan suggested. "I want to talk with those women."

"No, we can't yet," I told him. "We have a spelling bee to do first. The kids are in there. The news media are in there waiting for you." Boy, were they waiting.

"What are we supposed to do?" the vice president asked the event advance man.

"No big deal," he was assured. Just read words off the flash cards for the kids to spell. Another aide had even checked the cards prepared at the school. Can't be too cautious. No strange word to challenge the vice president in pronunciation. No politically incorrect word. No word with a potentially embarrassing double meaning. No hot potato. Or so the staff thought as Dan entered a room for the featured photo-op of the event—a campaign event, of course, and also an event to promote a worthy program, Weed and Seed.

Kids who were to display their spelling skills sat in the front rows. The news-media cameras were clustered in back. Dan was seated on a stool near the blackboard upon which kids would write the words they were given to spell. I was next to Dan. He started calling the youngsters to come forward to spell words listed on the flash cards. He would summon them, pointing, and voicing some description such as "The girl there in the red sweater." Three or four came forward to write their words correctly.

Dan and fame then summoned William Figueroa. The twelve-year-old sixth-grader wasn't from Munoz-Rivera School but was one of the kids from other nearby schools brought to participate in the nationally covered event.

"Potato," the vice president enunciated as the word for William. On the blackboard, William wrote "potato." Dan looked at the flash card. On the card was this spelling: "potatoe." Anxious to help the young man write letters to match those on the card, and certainly not really concentrating on the word, Dan offered an encouraging "You're close." He hinted that "you left a little something off." A man who presumably was one of the teachers suggested that William think of spelling "toe." Finally, reluctantly, William added an "e" to potato.

Applause greeted his "success." Applause was widespread in the room. No laughter. How many really had concentrated on spelling potato or had noticed the "e" error? Not many. I didn't. My mind then was on getting the vice president to the final events in the school, including making ice-cream sundaes with the kids in another spot, and finding time to get him outside to meet with the women in the neighborhood. We left the room unaware of any gaffe.

Though it put us behind schedule, we went as the vice president insisted, into the streets near the school so Dan finally could talk with those African American women. He wanted to ask them about the war on drugs and what could be done to keep the babies in their arms from growing up to become victims of gangs, drugs, and violence. Secret Service agents were going crazy. They had screened the neighborhood but had not specifically checked houses Dan went up to. Who was inside? They didn't know. The police chief expressed gratitude for the vice president's determination, nevertheless, to talk with people of the troubled neighborhood.

Ironically, at one porch we found a little kid about four years old holding a pistol. A water pistol. But you can imagine a Secret Service agent suddenly seeing a gun, even though it was quickly determined to be a toy.

The first I knew of a spelling problem was when a Quayle aide came up to me to say we "have an issue" at the school.

"What?"

"We misspelled potato," the anguished aide said.

"Who cares?" I responded.

"The media."

I still didn't get it. I didn't realize yet that the news media, counted on to tell the nation something about Weed and Seed, would instead ignore that entirely and feature only a gaffe that fit the image of a "dumb" Dan Quayle. So all the nation was told that the vice president had misspelled potato.

Most people never heard that Dan didn't actually add an "e." It was already on the card. Who added it? A teacher, presumably. Probably in haste in preparing for the spelling bee. Perhaps intending initially to have the word plural, "potatoes." A dirty trick? A plot to make Dan look bad? Spudgate? A prank? None of the above. This no doubt was just a bad break. Dan picked both the wrong card and the wrong kid.

William wasn't shy about describing the episode. In an interview with the *Trentonian*, the newspaper in Trenton, he said the episode made him believe the image of the vice president as "an idiot." Off William went for an appearance with David Letterman, where he suggested the vice president needed to study more. Not study CIA reports, I guess, but study for spelling bees.

Since so many Americans now get their political "news" from Letterman and Leno instead of from newspapers and network news—or at least they form opinions of political figures from the quips on those shows—the image problem was compounded. The news media were as harsh as the comedians. That night, all the news was about Quayle misspelling potato. Okay, it was fair game. Of course it would be reported, although more explanation of the origin of the added "e" could have been provided in fairness to the vice president.

My real disappointment was the lack of any coverage about Weed and Seed in the national news media. Where were the stories about successful programs at the school to save kids from drugs and gangs? Where were the accounts about Quayle going into the streets to talk with those women? Where was the balance?

Throughout the campaign, there was scant coverage of Weed and Seed, except for articles on some sports pages because of my association with basketball. This was not a sports story, however. Weed and Seed was a national initiative that was working and deserved attention.

Barbara Bush, in her book, *Reflections: Life after the White House*, lamented this lack of attention. She related how the late Jack Allin, former presiding bishop of the Episcopal Church of the USA and "our dear friend and summer minister," wrote to her during the campaign with concerns: "I remember he wrote me that he was distressed because he asked all his farmer friends about the Weed and Seed program that he had read about and not one of them had heard of it.

"Of course they hadn't!" the former First Lady continued. "The Weed and Seed program was run by former Notre Dame basketball coach Digger Phelps. It was an attempt to solve gang problems. Its goal was to weed out the gang leaders and seed the others out of gangs and into productive lives. It was a great program that never got the press attention it deserved."

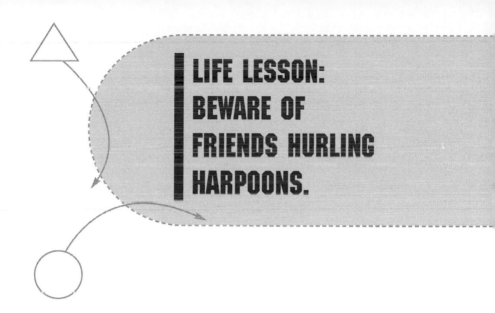

Chapter 17

Racing with Murphy Brown

"How did President Bush lose the 1992 election to Bill Clinton after being so popular after Desert Storm? Well, if I were analyzing it as a big basketball upset on *College Game Day* on ESPN, I'd say there were too many turnovers, too many mistakes by the Bush team, while the Clinton team followed a solid game plan to relentlessly attack an opponent's weakness: 'It's the economy, stupid.'"

Seventeen

In that 1992 campaign, President Bush wasn't running only against Bill Clinton, the Democratic nominee. Also in the race was Ross Perot, the quirky billionaire from Texas, an independent candidate who was taking more support away from Bush than from Clinton. And then we wound up running against *Murphy Brown* as well.

Murphy Brown was the name of a highly popular situation comedy on CBS. Candice Bergen played the role of Murphy, a TV anchor portrayed as a powerful, intelligent professional. Murphy was an unmarried woman making her way successfully in challenging situations. One challenge featured in the show was when Murphy became pregnant and had a child. No father had been identified in the episodes.

And then, in a speech on family values on May 19 in San Francisco, Dan Quayle uttered these words: "It doesn't help matters when primetime TV has Murphy Brown, a character who supposedly epitomizes today's intelligent, highly paid professional woman, mocking the importance of fathers by bearing a child alone and calling it just another lifestyle choice."

A raging controversy erupted. Alas, the Bush-Quayle ticket, sagging in the presidential polls, was seen as being in a contest with *Murphy Brown*, surging in the Nielsen ratings and especially popular with female viewers. What Dan was trying to stress about the importance of fathers was interpreted instead as an attack on single mothers and career women.

Dan didn't stand a chance in a race against Murphy. Taking her on made as much sense as my challenging Michael Jordan in a dunk competition. No way to win. I called George W. Bush, the president's son, who was working on his father's campaign, to express my concern that we were alienating whole groups of people that we didn't need to offend.

I say "we" because I was fully behind the reelection of my boss, the president. While I've always been a Democrat, I admired the good intentions, sincere efforts, and worthy goals of the president, who was a friend as well as a boss. He still is a friend. I still visit the former president and Barbara at Kennebunkport. I still admire him as a caring, compassionate man who has dedicated his life to public service, including World War II service as a navy pilot whose plane was shot down during one of many combat missions.

I'm a Reagan Democrat, voting mostly for Democrats but willing to split a ticket if Republicans offer what I consider a better choice for president. My boss and my friend was for me the better choice in '92.

"These campaign guys don't get it," I told George W. "The *Murphy Brown* speech hurt us. And your dad's in trouble." Then I ticked off some other mistakes, as I saw them, where Republican rhetoric was turning off environmentalists, gays, lesbians, blacks, immigrants, and other minority groups—and now single moms. Granted, some of those groups were not likely to vote heavily for the president. Nor, however, was it necessary to write them off or, worse, incite them to go to the polls in droves to defeat President Bush.

Weren't there gays and lesbians who favored conservative fiscal policy, who admired the president's success with Desert Storm, who might well for these or any number of other reasons vote for President Bush? Of course there were. Weren't there blacks who felt they were taken for granted by the Democratic Party, who understood that President Bush also deplored racism, who might also be attracted to vote for the president? Absolutely. Weren't there single mothers who also would consider voting for Bush? Certainly. Many. For many reasons.

But how many in any group will vote for you if your side is perceived as hostile, as bashing the whole group? My point was that if we kept alienating groups, who would be left to vote for us other than hard-core Republicans? Not enough. As Ronald Reagan showed, a Republican could appeal to many Democrats and independents, enough to turn a close election into a presidential landslide. Lose enough of them, and you turn what should be a landslide, based on the president's popularity after Desert Storm, into a presidential loss.

George W. understood what I was saying. Neither he nor his father wanted to turn off groups of voters. Although I didn't know George W. as well as I knew his father, we had a cordial relationship. Back before he was governor of Texas, George came often to Notre Dame football games with Joseph O'Neill Jr., a prominent Notre Dame alum from Texas, and his son, Joseph O'Neill III. They would drop by the basketball office. The younger O'Neill, now managing director of O'Neill Properties in Midland, Texas, and a Notre Dame trustee, is one of the best friends of George W. Then, when George W. was president of the Texas Rangers, pitcher Jamie Moyer, my son-in-law, was traded from the Cubs to the Rangers. On many a night, I'd sit in the owner's box and talk with George W. about the games of baseball, basketball, and politics.

Did I forecast back then that he someday would win the presidency? No. But then I don't always correctly forecast the winner of the NCAA Basketball Tournament either. In basketball, at least you can figure that all the players on a team are interested in the goal of winning. That's not always true in presidential politics.

The night after what was to become known as "the *Murphy Brown* speech," I met up with the Quayle campaign. Dan and Bill Kristol, the vice president's chief of staff, were talking about reaction to *Murphy Brown*. "Who?" I asked. I didn't know her. I had been used to watching game film rather than situation comedies if I was looking at a TV screen during primetime. So I didn't realize at first that they were talking about a TV show.

We watched tapes of news broadcasts. Wow! Dan vs. Murphy

was the big news. Representatives of women's causes responded with angry statements. Women around the country were calling talk shows and the White House switchboard. Most defended Murphy. Quite a few did not, but they were most likely already in the ranks of those certain to vote for the Bush-Quayle ticket. And already there were satirical remarks about the vice president debating a fictional character. The late-night comedians were to have a field day with that.

This was the headline in the New York *Daily News*: QUAYLE TO MURPHY BROWN: YOU TRAMP!

Critics hit at Dan's brief mention of Murphy as an attack on single mothers. Hillary Clinton, wife of the Democratic nominee, claimed it reflected the attitude of "an administration out of touch with America" and the increased number of single mothers. As I realized that *Murphy Brown* was that popular TV show and how the vice president's comment was being interpreted, I expressed my dismay to Quayle and Kristol.

They wondered, "Why are you so upset?"

My response: "Women vote!"

Now, let me be clear that Dan was absolutely right to express concern about the cultural damage from absentee fathers, from the abandonment of responsibility by men who father children and then choose to provide no love, no guidance, no role model, no support. Study after study shows the negative impact. And nobody aware of that impact now takes expression of concern about absentee fathers as an attack on single mothers. Also, Dan wasn't seeking to debate a popular TV character but rather to object to the way television was showing—or "mocking," in his view—the importance of fathers. He just did it in a way that ended up obscuring his point, leaving him open once more for ridicule.

The speech that angered so many women actually was written by a Quayle speechwriter who was herself an intelligent and successful professional woman. She clearly intended no attack on all those in her own category.

In an interview with CNN's Wolf Blitzer on the tenth anniversary of the *Murphy Brown* speech, Quayle described the controversial passage as "an eight-second deal in a forty-minute speech." He said his issue was not single motherhood but the absence of fathers, "that fathers need not be involved." He didn't back down from what he said and added that there had been "a lot of progress on the issue I tried to address." He tried. It didn't work. Murphy won. Of course.

We were burned in what Dan correctly described as "a firestorm." He also was correct in suggesting that the electronic media were rougher than the print media because "perhaps they felt I was attacking one of their own." Murphy, after all, was a TV anchor, even if a fictional one. Heck, he probably would have won more support if he had criticized one of the actual news anchors, all of whom had lower ratings than *Murphy Brown*.

How did President Bush lose the 1992 election to Bill Clinton after being so popular after Desert Storm? Well, if I were analyzing it as a big basketball upset on *College Game Day* on ESPN, I'd say there were too many turnovers, too many mistakes by the Bush team, while the Clinton team followed a solid game plan to relentlessly attack an opponent's weakness: "It's the economy, stupid."

Bush was a good president. My view, admittedly influenced by serving in his administration and having him as a friend, is that he could have been a great president in a second term. That's when he could have followed up on the success of Desert Storm with an Operation Domestic Storm, marshaling forces this time to fight problems at home, the problems we were beginning successfully to confront through Weed and Seed.

I had hoped for the proclaiming of a Domestic Storm in time to show voters the determination of the president to tackle our woes at home—with our schools, with our poorest neighborhoods, with drugs, with gangs, with preparing a workforce for global competition. That could have dispelled the false but harmful image that developed of Bush as unconcerned about the recession, about people hurt by a downturn in the economy.

At dinner with President and Barbara Bush before we flew the next day on *Air Force One* to South Bend for Bush's 1992 Notre Dame commencement speech, I told him of my confidence that a successful Domestic Storm rolling through the nation's troubled neighborhoods would be good for the country and good politics as well.

"I really believe in the Weed and Seed strategy," I told them. "If we can kick Saddam out of Kuwait, we can kick the negatives out of our own neighborhoods. It'll work. And we can sell this strategy to the American people." In the limousine on the way to the airport the next day, I again made a pitch to the president, predicting that with a successful Operation Weed and Seed alleviating so many of our long-neglected problems, "You will go down as one of the greatest presidents in this country's history."

Instead, he was to go down in defeat. No chance for doing this in a second term. If more emphasis had been put on finishing the first term with a storm rather than being on the defensive, maybe the president could have won reelection. We'll never know.

Barbara Bush was enthusiastic about such an effort. She wrote about it later in her book. The president was receptive as well. But he was beset, as presidents so often are, especially in a campaign year, with clamoring from special interests, Cabinet members, campaign strategists, editorial writers, TV commentators, and almost every other segment of the population for a host of priorities, many of which could neither be afforded nor even come close to winning Congressional approval. He cited Weed and Seed as a positive program but never was able to portray it as the storm for the future that we envisioned.

And the campaign gurus failed to get a focus on that opportunity, leaving the president vulnerable to the falsehood that he was doing nothing, was out of touch, and didn't even care. Contributing to the out-of-touch image was the absurd story that the president didn't even know there were scanners at supermarket checkout lines. That really was annoying and no doubt harmful. It came about when the president was shown new optical technology at a trade show. His interest in and apparent surprise at the new developments to speed the scanning and ensure greater accuracy was portrayed as surprise that there was such a thing as scanning at the checkout lines. Kind of like somebody registering surprise at the latest developments in TV screens and reception and being portrayed as not knowing that TV had gone beyond radio to provide pictures.

President Bush was so popular in 1991 after Desert Storm that his poll approval ratings hit an astounding 90 percent. He had brought together a coalition that threw Saddam Hussein out of Kuwait and crippled the dictator's forces, with minimum loss of life for our troops and with other nations sharing in the costs and cheering the success. (He also wisely listened to military advisors who warned against going on to occupy Iraq.)

Because Bush was so popular, the most prominent of the potential Democratic nominees for the '92 election decided not to run. Why bother? Wait for a race that can be won. Let somebody like that Arkansas governor be the sacrificial lamb. There'll be a better chance for another Democratic nominee to win in '96.

But the recession and problems with some of the president's fellow Republicans, ones who began the alienation of voters, led to plummeting in the polls. Ross Perot didn't help. Nor did the perceptions that the president was out of touch and aloof and that the popular Murphy Brown and single mothers in general had been labeled as tramps.

The recession actually was mild and officially was over before the 1992 election. The president knew that drastic actions some critics suggested weren't needed for recovery and would have hurt the economy in the long run. He was right. But it was Bill Clinton who was to inherit an economy ready to move ahead.

Lack of drastic action by Bush on the economy, however, fueled the contention that he wasn't concerned about the unemployed or underemployed and was only interested in foreign affairs. Knowing this perception, and how it was hurting the president's reelection chances, Clinton campaign strategist James Carville came up with the catchy, now-famous reminder for campaign focus: "It's the economy, stupid." It was brilliant strategy. Focus on a winning issue. Don't get sidetracked by flaps over side issues. Don't spend time and resources on matters most voters don't care about. What do they care most about? "It's the economy, stupid."

Some of the president's problems came not from the Carville strategy but the strategy of Republicans such as Pat Buchanan, the right-wing spieler who shifted back and forth between TV commentator and presidential candidate. Buchanan challenged Bush in the Republican primaries, forcing the president farther to the right politically to compete for conservative support that is vital in those primaries. The Buchanan challenges eroded some of the conservative base on which the president counted. And it forced the presidential appeal to the right, alienating many voters in the center—moderates, independents, Reagan Democrats. The center is where elections usually are won or lost.

Still, Buchanan was invited to give a speech at the Republican National Convention in Houston, where Bush and Quayle officially were nominated. It was a divisive speech proclaiming a cultural war and containing remarks that contributed to offending groups we did not need to write off as the enemy. Looking at it as a coach, I'd have told Buchanan to demonstrate teamwork or sit on the bench. Teamwork is vital in winning, whether we're talking sports or election campaigns.

While a lot of convention stridency turned off voters, there also was a speech with a different appeal, an appeal that made me proud to be, not a Republican, but a Reagan Democrat. Ronald Reagan, in a farewell speech, said this: "Whatever else history may say about me when I'm gone, I hope it will record that I appealed to your best hopes, not your worst fears, to your confidence rather than your doubts."

Sure, Reagan had some partisan remarks. It was, after all, the Republican Convention. But he used humor rather than vituperation to make his points. He expressed the "fondest hope for each one of you," not just for those who agreed with all of his governmental philosophy. He spoke of inclusiveness and proclaimed, "Whether we come from poverty or wealth; whether we are Afro-American or Irish-American, Christian or Jewish, from big cities or small towns, we are all equal in the eyes of God." This was inclusiveness with which to win. A race with *Murphy Brown* was not.

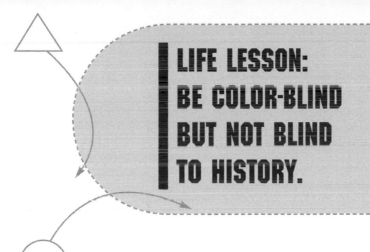

Chapter 18

Foreign Policy: Is the President Naked Underneath?

"It was good to see the bad. We need to see reality, not just what will be fun or pleasant. And, although I didn't realize it when I expressed a desire to see more than just the niceties of an inauguration, it helped us in our goal of better relations with the new government. We were told that most of the other foreign delegations just hung out at their hotel, at the bar, at the pool, or at the beach. We were praised for our interest in the country and our effort to understand."

Eighteen

Back when I was trying unsuccessfully just to find a high school coaching job, never did I imagine that one day I would be engaged in foreign diplomacy. Nor did anybody who knew me.

But there I was early in January of 1993, Digger the diplomat, representing the United States in Ghana in a very touchy situation, the presidential inauguration of Jerry Rawlings, a revolutionary who had led a military revolt and now was to serve as an elected leader. Some in our State Department seemed to view him as a looming Saddam Hussein of that day. They feared he would be a dictator, ruthless in stifling opposition, who never would willingly relinquish power. But other nations, especially Japan, were seeking cordial relations with Rawlings to enhance their influence and trade prospects in that area of Africa. Their gain could be our loss.

President Bush, though defeated in the 1992 election, still was the president and responsible for our foreign policy when he named me in December of that year as head of our delegation to the Rawlings inauguration in January, shortly before our own inaugural change to President Clinton.

Why me? To me, it was a presidential vote of confidence, an indication of his trust in me as a result of my performance with Operation Weed and Seed. While that service enabled me to demonstrate skills beyond coaching players to position for a rebound, this assignment was more than just domestic diplomacy. I would represent the president, indeed, the nation, in a foreign land of historic significance for America.

Ghana had been a center for the slave trade, a land to which many African-Americans trace their roots. And this was another reason I was selected by President Bush. Throughout my life, I always had a positive relationship with African-Americans, from being the only white kid playing basketball with black friends in Beacon to recruiting black athletes for Notre Dame and then more recently going into some of the most troubled predominately black neighborhoods to work with the people to weed and seed, to bring the economic opportunity so lacking long after Lincoln's Emancipation Proclamation. And the president knew I'd seek all the information I could find and prepare a game plan for the event. So, I thought that sending me to Ghana made sense. I was to find that Jerry Rawlings thought so, too.

While I scoured briefings on Rawlings and Ghana, I admit I wasn't prepared for the style of travel, flying on an official aircraft that looked as impressive as *Air Force One*, what with the same blue and white colors and lettering designating "United States of America." I joked to the other five members of the delegation that I guess we were flying "United." Or was it "American?"

On the way, we landed at an Air Force base in the Azores to refuel. As we taxied toward the tower, I saw these dozen people lined up, saluting. I'm thinking, "What the hell are they doing out there?" As we start to get off the plane, they're still there, still saluting. I was told I'm supposed to be the last one off. Okay, I guess this has something to do with leading the delegation. I'm on the ground. And they're still saluting. I look back, and sure enough, there's nobody else getting off. Believe it or not, they were saluting me, the undertaker's son from Beacon. This was a part of heading an official United States delegation that I sure wasn't prepared for at all.

A general comes over and introduces himself. "Hi, general, it's Digger," I said. "Let's go get a beer." No, he said, he was there for the formal greeting that they provide "any time a blue and white [official plane] comes in."

In Ghana, I wanted to see some of the country, the villages and the average folks and how they lived, not just see an inaugural ceremony and the important officials. Although I knew it would not be a fun experience, I especially wanted to see Cape Coast Castle, where so many of the ancestors of our African-American population set sail in chains for slavery.

We traveled to some villages. At one, I was startled to find that I was to be made an honorary tribal chief. It was very impressive. Very nice of them. And I deeply appreciated it. Not because I could call myself Chief Digger but because of what it symbolized in terms of their desire for friendship between our peoples.

We visited with Peace Corps workers. Ghana was the first country in the world to welcome the Peace Corps in 1961, shortly after its creation in the administration of John F. Kennedy. We saw firsthand the infrastructure problems. Roads. Sewers. The need for improvements was obvious. We went to a trade school in Accra. The efforts for improving education were obvious.

Then we went to see the sprawling white structure on the sea called the Cape Coast Castle. More aptly, perhaps, it should be called the Cape Coast Dungeon. It was the biggest of the slave-trading centers on the coastline of what now is Ghana. While it was also a fortified castle, with rows of ancient cannons still pointing to the sea, beneath the fortifications were the dungeons, the men's dungeon and the women's dungeon, where many of the ancestors of our African-Americans were held in what must have been terrible conditions. No sanitation. No fresh air. No room. No hope.

These hapless captives often had been taken as prisoners in tribal war and turned over for a slave trade that can be traced back to Roman times and even before. They were packed like sardines awaiting the ships on which they would be loaded for a trip to a far-off land in which they never would be able to contact the mothers, fathers, children, siblings, and friends from whom they were taken.

A museum now is located in the castle, providing information and exhibits about those awful times. Comment books enable visitors—many are African-Americans drawn back in a quest for their roots—to write about their feelings. Some leave notes: Notes with words of prayer for ancestors they never knew. Notes with sadness. Notes with anger. Notes expressing hope that such inhumanity will never be permitted again.

A tour took us to what is labeled the "Door of No Return." Two enormous black doors under an arched doorway open to show the path to the sea along which captives were herded like cattle to the slave ships.

It was good to see the bad. We need to see reality, not just what will be fun or pleasant. And although I didn't realize it when I expressed a desire to see more than just the niceties of an inauguration, it helped us in our goal of better relations with the new government. We were told that most of the other foreign delegations just hung out at their hotel, at the bar, at the pool, or at the beach. We were praised for our interest in the country and our effort to understand.

We went as well to the formal events, as expected, including a reception at the presidential residence. Ironically, it also had once been one of the slave castles. A couple of Ghanaians came up to me at the reception. "Digger, what are you doing here?" one of them asked.

I told him I was heading the U.S. delegation for the inauguration and then looked puzzled at how these two guys knew me. They were friends of President Rawlings, and they had gone to college in America, at UCLA. Yep, you can bet that students at UCLA of their era knew me. These guys were kind in their remarks. They appreciated our basketball competition and were pleased that the delegation was headed by somebody they knew rather than an assistant undersecretary in charge of parking garages in the District of Columbia.

The day after the inauguration, we were to meet briefly with President Rawlings. He could have snubbed us. Our ambassador still had not yet even presented his credentials. Our State Department had not been enthused about Rawlings, to say the least. Understandably, there had been concern.

Rawlings was a revolutionary. He was an air force flight lieutenant who led a coup in 1979—actually two attempts that year, the second one successful. He had become upset with what he regarded as a fledgling democracy gone astray in Ghana. He railed against social injustice, the rise of a privileged class, and the demoralization of the military, where power rested in the fragile new democracy.

He took control of the country, seemed at times to be a leftist turning toward the Soviet Union, and then disappointed his leftist supporters by embracing Western ideals. He dared to hold a 1992 presidential election. He won. Fair election? I don't know. I wasn't there as an observer. Some people don't think our presidential elections are totally fair, especially when the Electoral College can keep the candidate with the most votes from winning. And my assignment had nothing to do with advocating different election procedures in Ghana or protesting what was a fact: Rawlings was president.

When we met the new president, he at first expressed anger at his treatment by the United States. No surprise. I had been briefed on the prospect of a rather short, unproductive session. "Why did your country want to low-profile your representation [at the inauguration] until Digger was involved?" he asked our delegation. Whew, at least he thought I had enhanced our prestige.

"Didn't your country have a revolution?" Rawlings asked. "Didn't your country have George Washington, who was a military man, a revolutionary like me?

"You killed a lot of people during that revolution with the British," Rawlings said, seeking to answer State Department criticism about deaths in his quest to change the government in Ghana through revolution.

"I love my country," Rawlings said with emotion that seemed to me to be sincere. "I want my country to work."

Rawlings had been briefed, too. He was aware of my coaching and my reputation for working with African-Americans in positive ways. I wondered if his friends from UCLA also had put in a good word for me. He apparently was pleased that President Bush had sent me to head the delegation.

The ice broken, we started talking about economic development, infrastructure, transportation, health, prospects for tourism. We acknowledged problems faced by Ghana and problems I faced with Weed and Seed. We are just talking one-on-one with friendly informality. He's calling me "Digger." I'm calling him "Jerry" after the initial "Mr. President" formality.

There are over seventy countries waiting to see this guy before they leave. Japan is next after us, waiting. As our fifteen-minute meeting extends to forty-five minutes, I'm thinking in the back of my mind, "Boy, this isn't going to go over well with the Japanese delegation."

As we finally get ready to leave, I present the traditional gift from President Bush for such an occasion. Rawlings in turn has a gift for me to take back to Bush. It was a kente-cloth garment, a colorful cloth with bold designs that is worn on special occasions. Rawlings turns to one of his aides and says, "Go get one for Digger, too." The aide returns with a beautiful cloth.

"How do you put it on?" I asked, honestly baffled. So he shows me how to wrap it around. I'm wearing a business suit. Not what is supposed to be underneath the wrap. In fact, I didn't think anything went underneath. "I noticed the day before the inauguration you were wearing one of these," I said. "Do you go naked underneath?"

"Like the Irish with their kilts?" I persisted. The president, so angry at the start, now is laughing loudly, especially at me with my kente cloth wrapped around a business suit. By now everybody is laughing (except, no doubt, for the waiting Japanese delegation).

As we finally left, all in a good mood and laughing, we passed the waiting Japanese, who had been so hopeful of benefiting from expected hostility by Rawlings toward the United States. They were fried. You could tell. Fried to a crisp. They stared at me, with looks of displeasure.

"Hey, talk to the main man," I said.

My hope was to play some small part in establishing better relations.

Rawlings later was to host President Clinton and Queen Elizabeth, both impressed by his efforts as an elected president to encourage economic and democratic stability. He was reelected in 1996 to a second term and then, as the constitution provided, stepped aside after two terms. There was a peaceful transition, even though the opposition party won the 2000 election over his choice for president.

I'd be proud to wear the ceremonial kente cloth he gave me. Not with a business suit this time. But with something underneath, especially during a cold South Bend winter.

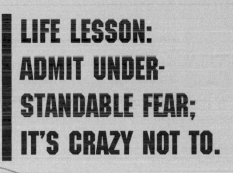

Chapter 19

Voting in the Killing Fields

"Yes, I readily admit fear. Anyone in that situation who claimed not to be afraid would be crazy or a liar or some combination thereof. Khmer Rouge guerrillas still were active and intent on sabotaging the elections. A Japanese civilian policeman assigned to the U.N. peacekeeping force had been killed and another critically wounded in a rocket attack. Seven other Japanese and Dutch peacekeepers had been wounded in an ambush of a U.N. convoy."

Nineteen

Even this undertaker's son, growing up with death all around, learning out of necessity to be somewhat calloused to it, was shaken, choked up, by the sight of the Killing Fields of Cambodia.

In the spring of 1993, I went to Cambodia as a United Nations observer for the first multiparty elections in that troubled nation in decades, the first vote since the genocide inflicted on the gentle people of Cambodia by Pol Pot, leader of the Khmer Rouge. He was the Hitler of his time. Also, Cambodia had been occupied by Vietnam, a mixed blessing. The Vietnamese drove the horrible Khmer Rouge from power but then stayed on as an occupying force until the United Nations stepped in to seek restoration of Cambodia as a free, independent nation.

An American diplomat who is a Notre Dame graduate talked me into volunteering as an election observer. Sure to be interesting, I thought. A way to be of service after leaving Weed and Seed and wanting still to contribute, if not in the streets of our cities, then for a time in the cause of world peace.

Interesting it was. I was quoted by the Associated Press in an interview in Cambodia as saying the experience ranks right up there with breaking UCLA's eighty-eight-game winning streak but with much more at stake. "But let's face it," I said, "basketball is just a game."

The losers in the Killing Fields lost more than a game; they lost their lives. Nobody knows the exact death toll. Estimates of the number of people killed outright or starved, tortured, or worked to death during the brutal Khmer Rouge regime range from about 1.7 million to as many as 2 million. Over a quarter of the population perished after the Khmer Rouge, a communist guerrilla force, took power in Phnom Penh, the capital of Cambodia, on April 17, 1975. The monster Pol Pot and his zealots, seeking an agrarian society, forced city dwellers into the countryside or into labor camps.

The Killing Fields were fields littered with bodies of the victims, people killed because they were deemed too educated to be indoctrinated, too old to work, too slow to respond to a command, too weak from near starvation to be productive, too sympathetic toward other victims being hauled away, or too different in ethnic background. Or a victim could be someone for whom an overbearing, angry teenage Khmer Rouge soldier took a dislike for any reason or no reason at all.

Walking in those fields where bones of the unidentified remained scattered about drove home the stark contrast between those deaths—with undignified, unceremonial, uncaring dumping of bodies—and the dignity, care, and compassion in a funeral conducted by my father in Beacon. Family and friends of Pol Pot victims could not gather to grieve, to pay respects, or to recall favorite memories. They could not know for sure if, where, or when a relative had been killed. They usually knew only that the person had been taken away. They came of course to presume death. But they could not visit a gravesite.

A memorial has been established. Skulls have been amassed for display. Many have cracks or holes, damage inflicted in a clubbing that was the final blow of death. There was no perfection in embalming of the type my father sought. No embalming. Just discarding in those fields. The memorial is horrible to view, but a necessary reminder to the rest of the world that it should not again turn away as genocide reigns anew elsewhere. That lesson, unfortunately, has not been learned. The world looked away again in ignoring genocide in Darfur.

Anyone who has not seen the outstanding, award-winning 1984 motion picture on this genocide, *The Killing Fields*, should do so. It is powerful, moving, but not quite as moving as seeing the actual bones and skulls of victims.

My task in Cambodia as a representative of the United Nations Transitional Authority in Cambodia (UNTAC) was to help the nation achieve independence and a democratic rather than a despotic rule through free and fair elections. I was assigned to a polling station in the poor, isolated town of Daung in the eastern province of Svay Rieng. We were a mile from the Vietnam border. My backup plan, my escape route, was to race that mile to the border if the Khmer Rouge attacked the polling station. Could I have outrun a Khmer Rouge bullet? I don't know. But the damn thing would have known it was in a race.

I was dropped off alone, instructed to supervise a twenty-one-member Cambodian election team, none of whom spoke a word of English. And I speak Cambodian as well as I speak Martian. The assignment was to make sure that all was ready for the six days of voting—from May 23 through May 28—and that procedures for conducting a fair U.N.-sanctioned election were followed.

A sinking feeling enveloped me when I saw the small building designated as a polling place. Actually, I was afraid it would be the voters who would sink. Heavy rains had left the field in front of the building flooded. That's where voters—if many of them came—would have to stand in line to cast their ballots. Also, we feared, the simmering sun could discourage voters from waiting very long to vote. After all, in the United States, it would be unthinkable to walk through a flooded field to vote. Heck, even a light rain holds down our turnout. And voters here sometimes turn away when they see a line for voting, even a line inside a climate-controlled structure. The field dried, luckily, and we affixed blue awning-type material outside to provide shade, just in case the voters came in numbers to create lines.

Well, there was no Holiday Inn nearby. No place at all to stay, except in a mud and brick elementary school. My "bed" was a desk inside a storage shack with a tile roof. It heated up like an oven under the blistering sun and didn't much cool off at night, when mosquitoes swarmed and dove like squadrons of dive-bombers to attack. Thank heavens for the mosquito net and malaria shots. Sleep was difficult. Mosquitoes, a lumpy desk, strange sounds in the night, and fear that the Khmer Rouge would come to blow up the voting station were distractions. All this allowed maybe three hours of sleep.

Yes, I readily admit fear. Anyone in that situation who claimed not to be afraid would be crazy or a liar or some combination thereof. Khmer Rouge guerrillas still were active and intent on sabotaging the elections. A Japanese civilian policeman assigned to the U.N. peacekeeping force had been killed and another critically wounded in a rocket attack. Seven other Japanese and Dutch peacekeepers had been wounded in an ambush of a U.N. convey.

For a while there were fears that Japan might withdraw all its soldiers and civilians who were heavily involved in the peacekeeping. That would have been a blow to chances of successfully conducting the elections. Indian peacekeepers also had been attacked and wounded. And there was a report of nearly three hundred Khmer Rouge guerrillas firing on U.N. soldiers and briefly seizing an airport in another area.

Strange sounds in the night, indeed. Was that one of the restless pigs or chickens that made themselves at home at the school? Was that just the wind? Was that the call of some animal in the nearby jungle? Or could it be a Khmer Rouge guerrilla sneaking up to greet a U.N. observer?

We also were alerted to possible voter intimidation efforts by the government's political party. With illiteracy so high in this area, with the population so worn down by war and poverty, with these circumstances of violence and intimidation, would anybody come to vote?

What happened was astounding. By 5:30 that Sunday morning, women from the rice fields and nearby villagers began streaming to the polling place, lining up two and a half hours before the polls opened. First in line was a woman who was terribly nervous, scared. She certainly was aware of the threats and fearful that voting could be costly, costing jobs held by her family, perhaps costing her life. When she finally put her ballot in the box and began to walk away, I looked into her face. It said it all. There was pride and gratitude and hope for the future. She didn't have to say a word. Even if she had, I wouldn't have known what she said. But I understood the look in her eyes, on her face. I just choked up and said to myself, "That's why I'm here, to help stop the killing and bring peace for people like that woman." I've never seen such determination.

All day they came. Lines extended well beyond the area where we had affixed the blue awning to provide some shade. They didn't seem to mind the blazing sun. They were determined to vote and they did. When the voting ended on the following Friday, about 95 percent of the five thousand registered voters in the Daung area had cast their ballots. Our voter turnouts, even in what we call a "heavy" vote in the 2004 presidential election, pale by comparison.

Since there was not the convenience of absentee ballots, an old man, very ill, was hauled to the polling place on the back of a motorcycle. He was so weak, however, that he could not alight to enter the voting area. So I violated the election rules. I took the ballot box to him. If that was election fraud, I'm proud to have committed it. I'm not a "rules is rules" guy when common sense and doing what is right dictates a little flexibility. People who preach that every law should be followed without question in all circumstances ought to turn themselves in to the police and ask for a ticket the next time they accidentally go 31 miles an hour in a 30 speed zone.

As I looked at the line of people awaiting a chance to vote, I noticed that most were women. Were the men not as concerned about voting? "Where are the men?" I asked an interpreter who had come for the voting.

"Dead," he said, looking at me as though I should have known. And I should have. There were younger men and some older men, but entire generations of men who would by then have been in middle age had been killed.

Duties extended to safeguarding ballots and supervision of tabulation, a lengthy process over days. No immediate declaring of victors as usually happens in this country. The ruling Cambodian

People's Party, which had been installed by Vietnam and sought through intimidation to retain power, lost the election, triggering claims by the government of voting irregularities. U.N. officials declared, however, that the election was free and fair. In the area I supervised, I agreed with that observation wholeheartedly. What happened as a result of the vote might not be in accord with our ideas of how democracy should function, but not every country wants or needs a government and democratic election system just like ours. Sometimes we forget that. We certainly did in Iraq.

A royalist party with the long name National United Front for an Independent, Neutral, Peaceful and Cooperative Cambodia got the most votes and won the most seats, fifty-eight, in the new 120-member National Assembly. The People's Party won fifty-one seats. After some tense negotiations involving a royal-family feud and threats of civil war and possible reemergence of the Khmer Rouge, the assembly finally approved a democratic constitution and proclaimed the long-revered and often-unpredictable Prince Norodom Sihanouk, then seventy, as king. Thus, Sihanouk returned as king and head of government twenty-three years after he was ousted in a U.S.-backed coup.

Now, the United States quickly recognized his government. The choice of the election-winning royalist party and the only leader acceptable to virtually all factions, even the Khmer Rouge, had been selected. Full-scale civil war was averted. Cambodia was independent. While problems and conflicts remained, the Killing Fields have not been planted anew with more indented skulls.

I was proud to have played a part in this success in my one corner of that nation. Also, in seeing what had happened in Cambodia and studying why, I came to appreciate more the role of this country in foreign policy, sometimes for good, sometimes not, even though our intentions may always seem to our foreign policy and military officials to be worthy.

Still visible were the huge craters from bombs dropped from B-52s in the so-called "secret war" in Cambodia, an effort to halt the flow of supplies by North Vietnam through the eastern edge of Cambodia to its regulars and the Viet Cong in

South Vietnam. Did this hardly secret effort unintentionally help the Khmer Rouge? And did we later show support for that terrible group because it was opposing Vietnam's invasion?

Sometimes there are unintended consequences, such as in ousting Saddam Hussein but, in doing so, removing a buffer against expansion of Iran's influence. If the United States organized the coup to oust Sihanouk—at least the coup results were favored, if not actually engineered—did that lead to unintended consequences in Cambodia?

Watch out for what you wish in foreign policy. Sometimes you get the wish and later rue the consequences.

Yugoslavia, too, is an example.

Some nations in Europe wished for success of their favorite sides as Yugoslavia was breaking up in 1990, going beyond wishing to provide encouragement and assistance for breaking away. If they didn't promote a breakup, they stood by as it occurred, only to be appalled soon thereafter by the horror of bloody conflicts and ethnic cleansing.

The United States acted nobly and effectively with other nations in Bosnia and Kosovo. However, the peacekeeping came belatedly.

Because of my frequent trips to Yugoslavia with my Notre Dame teams and on my own, with an eye on recruiting and also on the potential and beauty of Yugoslavia, I was convinced that the breakup horrors did not have to occur.

Tito held the country together by force of personality and dictatorial powers. Economics could have held it together without need for a dictator, if the powerful nations of the world had provided assistance for economic development and encouragement to stay together and work together.

Yugoslavia could have become the Hong Kong of the Baltic and Mediterranean. Parts of it still could. Help in pursuing that development, mostly through investment, would have cost the powerful nations less than the higher price later of sending military forces to intervene and provide for peacekeeping and restoration.

Would there still have been ethnic differences? Of course. Could some parts still have broken away? Yes. Remember all the differences there were among the parts that became the United States, differences that eventually led to the Civil War? Development of an economy of mutual benefit to all the states and wise leadership showed how diverse parts can become a united country.

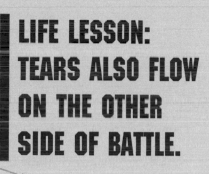

Chapter 20

A Russian I Couldn't Kill

"'Serg,' I said. 'Let me tell you something. If we ever go to war, I can't kill you. If you and I go head to head and I've got a rifle, I can't pull the trigger. You're my friend. I don't care what's going on politically. When it comes back to the people like you and me, to the people at the grass-roots of our countries, we get along fine. It's the politicians and the policies that create the monsters that are out there. And then we have to defend those policies.'

He was smiling, nodding in agreement."

Twenty

Sergei Belov ranks as one of the greatest basketball players in the world—ever. He led the Russian National Team to numerous championships in international competition from 1968 to 1980. Included was the 1972 Olympic victory in Munich over the United States in a gold-medal game tarnished by controversy over decisions by the referees to put time back on the clock three times after what appeared to have been a one-point victory for the U.S.A. But Sergei didn't put time back, and he didn't score that final basket for a one-point Russian victory. That was the big forward, Aleksander Belov.

But Sergei was the magician with the ball at guard who brought the Russian team to international prominence. They were either a point better than the U.S.A. or just a point behind, if the clock resetting was improper. Never before had this country, where basketball was invented, lost an Olympic basketball game. That type of dominance is of course no more. But back then, there was the belief in this country that our top college players could easily overcome the semipro basketball teams of other nations.

Sergei was a colonel in the Red Army. And once I talked about shooting him. Actually, about not shooting him. We became friends. Our mutual interests included stamp collecting as well as basketball. Twice his Russian National Team played exhibition games with my Notre Dame teams. And often we sent messages back and forth and even exchanged small gifts and new postage stamps issued in our countries.

On my mantel today is a beautiful replica of a Russian Orthodox church given to me by Sergei. He knew I was a Roman Catholic and wanted to give me something from Russia with religious meaning, despite the efforts of communism back then to deny the validity of religion.

We exchanged stamps that our countries issued on space exploration. And when the Russian National Team sought to retain its Olympic championship at the games in Montreal in 1976, Sergei asked Bill Guthridge, an assistant coach of the United States team, to bring back stamps from Russia for me. Bill was also an assistant at the University of North Carolina for Dean Smith, who that year coached the Olympic team in its quest to return to gold-medal form. Sergei didn't even ask for the stamps back after the U.S.A., led in scoring by Adrian Dantley, my star Notre Dame player, won the championship undefeated. Two of Bob Knight's Indiana University players, Scott May and Quinn Buckner, also played key roles, as did North Carolina's Phil Ford. Russia that time got the bronze medal for third.

The talk about shooting, with rifles rather than with basketballs, came after the visit by Sergei and his Russian teammates for an exhibition game at Notre Dame. We already were friends and had swapped stamps and basketball stories. He spoke English quite well. Good thing. Otherwise there would have been no verbal communication. After the game, I showed Sergei around campus and around South Bend and drove him back to the inn where his team was staying. We had even talked a little politics, about the differences in the political systems in our countries and the resulting fears of military conflict in those Cold War days.

"Serg," I said. "Let me tell you something. If we ever go to war, I can't kill you. If you and I go head to head and I've got a rifle, I can't pull the trigger. You're my friend. I don't care what's going on politically. When it comes back to the people like you and me, to the people at the grassroots of our countries, we get along fine. It's the politicians and the policies that create the monsters that are out there. And then we have to defend those policies."

He was smiling, nodding in agreement.

"But, Serg, here's what we can do," I suggested. "If the politicians and policies get us into a war, why don't we just get a case of beer and go hide in the mountains? And when it's over and one side claims victory over what's left of the world, if I've got to be a communist, I'll be a communist. If you've got to be a capitalist, you're a capitalist. More importantly, whatever we call ourselves, we're brothers."

He knew what I was saying. He knew the point I was making, even if the Red Army colonel and I never would have wound up in the mountains amidst the horrors of nuclear war. He agreed with the philosophy of the peoples of the world seeking brotherhood rather than the warfare brought on by the mistakes and miscalculations of politicians.

My thoughts about the death of those who serve in the military go back to childhood memories of military funerals I witnessed as the son of an undertaker and eventually an assistant in the family business. An honor guard would come up from West Point. The solemn ceremony included folding the American flag that had covered the coffin and presenting it to the mother of a soldier who had died in Korea or somewhere else while in the service of his country. There would be a twenty-one-gun salute. And the tears. So many tears. Another mother leaving the cemetery in grief, undoubtedly to return to the grave in weeks, months, and years to come to weep again and again. I would feel so sorry. And I wondered, does this go on in other countries where soldiers fighting for some other cause lose their lives and their mothers lose their sons?

Once, I recall asking a nun at St. John's Church, where I went as a child for religious instruction, about what happened when German soldiers were killed during World War II. As kids, we played soldiers, always on the "right" side, always defeating the enemy. We knew that Catholic soldiers fighting for God and country on our side would go to Heaven if they were killed in combat.

"What about the Germans?" I asked the nun. "Were there Germans who were Catholic? If they got killed fighting against us, did they go to Heaven?" I wondered too if there had been

German mothers crying, grieving just like the mothers I saw. The good sister, startled, and with what I recall as a "wow" expression, sought to provide a brief explanation but did not welcome pursuing the subject that should not have been raised by a kid so young. But I was a kid who was an undertaker's son.

It's always bothered me. I wonder why so often there are those tragic situations in which soldiers die, not because they even know the people shooting at them or the people at whom they shoot. It's because they grew up in a country in which they were expected to serve at a time of war. Was the cause just or just a miscalculation? Was it just because of some dictator's lust for power?

And I wonder even more now as old enemies who once sought to kill each other join to embrace, literally, as they return to old battlefields. We see photos of Americans and Vietnamese embracing now at the Vietnam War Memorial. We read of American veterans of World War II battles meeting with their counterparts from Germany or Japan. Even former prisoners of war, such as Senator John McCain, who suffered so much for so long in Vietnamese custody, return to the land of their captors to talk of peaceful pursuits of trade and cultural exchange. They talk there with folks who once fled bombs dropped from our planes.

If those who sought to kill each other can forgive and embrace, why couldn't the wars in which they fought have been avoided by some forgiveness, compromise, and negotiation? Is it easier to shoot and kill and later find forgiveness than it would be to find forgiveness first to prevent shooting and killing?

The forgiveness after war comes too late, of course, for those who were killed and for their grieving mothers and other relatives and friends.

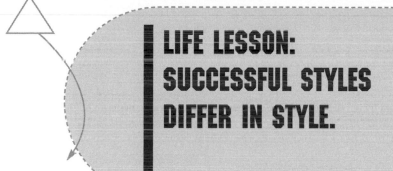

Chapter 21

Bob Knight and Al McGuire: On Court and Off

"No coach is better organized than Bob Knight. Nor is there a better teacher. He prepares a team superbly in practices, teaching the game as it should be played, demanding perfection on defense as well as offense. He seeks to motivate each player to reach his potential. He is a tough disciplinarian, requiring his players to go to class, act right, play hard, and work together as a team. He has put all that together to produce championship teams, including one of the greatest, his Indiana University team that won all thirty-two games and the national championship in 1975–76."

Twenty-one

In addition to my immediate family in Beacon, my mom, dad, and sisters, I had two "brothers" in coaching, Bob Knight and Al McGuire. They were like brothers, helping me, sometimes with advice, sometimes by example, sometimes by just being a friend. Knight and McGuire, though far different in coaching styles, personalities, and public images, share outstanding, winning records that include building and leading teams to national championships.

I knew Bob first. We go way back to when we both attended a basketball clinic while I was a volunteer graduate assistant at Rider College and Bob was an assistant coach at Army. We became friends, talking basketball, playing golf, and hoping for successful careers in coaching. Neither of us had much money. Since Bob was at West Point, so close to Beacon, I told him that my dad would hire him to work funerals, pay twenty bucks for driving the hearse or being a pallbearer. Bob would have been a good pallbearer, strong enough to help with the heaviest of caskets, serious enough in natural facial expression for ideal funeral service and organized enough to please my perfectionist dad. But he never took this opportunity.

No coach is better organized than Bob Knight. Nor is there a better teacher. He prepares a team superbly in practices, teaching the game as it should be played, demanding perfection on defense as well as offense. He seeks to motivate each player to reach his potential. He is a tough disciplinarian, requiring his players to go to class, act right, play hard, and work together as a team.

He has put all that together to produce championship teams, including one of the greatest, his Indiana University team that won all thirty-two games and the national championship in 1975–76.

Our friendship continued as we competed, Knight at IU, me at Notre Dame. We stressed similar principles, not just on the court but in recruiting and in admonishing the kids to attend class, get good grades, stay out of trouble, go on to graduate, and become useful citizens. IU won thirteen of the eighteen games we played. That in itself is ample reason for me to conclude that Bob is a great coach. The five wins all were satisfying, coming against some of his best teams. One of the most significant to me was the game we won in Bloomington two years after we lost 94–29 there in that rout during my first season.

Bob and I had disdain for colleges that violated NCAA rules repeatedly to cheat in recruiting. We would not break the rules no matter what good prospect we might lose to other coaches "bidding" for that player. We were proud that our schools wanted no cheating. Notre Dame then and now demands that its coaches recruit the right way. IU at that time also wanted a coach who would never violate NCAA regulations.

Knight was fired at IU after Myles Brand, then the university president and later NCAA president, declared that Knight had violated a "zero tolerance" for displays of temper. If a university president wants to find a reason to replace a coach, the reason will of course be found. I learned that lesson.

Bob did have some public displays of temper. Most coaches do. The one always cited by his critics is when he tossed a chair in a 1985 game against Purdue. Bob says he just saw an old lady standing behind the basket and tossed her a chair. True? No. But Bob will joke even at his own expense.

Did Bob use some bad language directed at his players? Certainly. Most coaches do. Can you image getting the attention of a hulking, macho, nineteen-year-old college athlete by saying, "Gracious, son, I sure do wish, if you don't mind, that you would remember to block out for those rebounds."

IU's loss was Texas Tech's gain. In his first year coaching there, Bob turned around a poor program, going 23–9 and finishing tied for third in the Big 12. The prior year, Texas Tech had been 9–19 and eleventh in the conference. Bob has a compassionate side that does not come to public attention. He is loyal to his friends. He never forgets the contributions of his former coaches and the great coaches of past eras who developed the game. He cares about and helps his former players.

I was staying at Bob's house in Bloomington on the night of November 21, 1991, when my daughter Karen telephoned with the news that my dad had died. As an undertaker's son, I had been around death, getting used to it as a part of life. But to see someone so close die is something different. I did not want to be there when my dad died. I knew he was really sick, with a debilitating blood disease related to formaldehyde poisoning from his decades of embalming. When I visited him in late October, it was heartbreaking to see him in such deteriorating health, to see him suffering. We placed a bed for him in the TV room, right next to the kitchen. It took him five minutes just to make it to the kitchen for half a banana or half a glass of orange juice. The struggle was difficult, tiring, painful, and disheartening.

And so I went to the little chapel of the Capuchin Franciscans at Beacon, a place very special to me. I lit a candle, looked at Jesus on the Cross, looked at the statue of the Blessed Mother, and prayed: "Please take him. He's had enough. He can't get any better. He doesn't need this anymore."

Since I knew I couldn't handle being present, knew I'd be of no value to those who were there, I tried to get wrapped up in other things, to get away. That's why I was at Bob's house when the news came. I went to Bloomington for his practice that afternoon. At his house that evening we planned to break down the tape of his team's recent loss to UCLA in the Tip-off Classic. I wanted to get wrapped up in helping Bob in order to find at least brief relief from the mental anguish over my father's deteriorating condition.

Karen's call came: "Dad, Papa died." Even though I expected it—had even prayed for it—the finality of it, the realization that the undertaker's son no longer had the father he loved, struck hard. I was distraught and wanted only to jump in my car to drive back to South Bend to bring the family together and get a private plane to take us to Beacon for the funeral.

Bob wouldn't let me leave. He couldn't have been nicer. Couldn't have been more understanding. He said I was in no condition emotionally to go on a late-night trip on some lousy roads. He was right. I listened. Got a little sleep. Left early in the morning, traveling in daylight. I cried all the way. But I got there safely and more prepared for the funeral preparations, including a eulogy that I wanted to deliver in a way that would do justice to the memory of my dad.

There have been times when Bob listened to me. One time was in 1984, when he was the coach of the U.S. Olympic basketball team. The games were in Los Angeles. I was there with ABC to work with Keith Jackson on the telecasts. Knight, in his typical way, sought to honor the achievements of legendary coach Hank Iba by having him as an honorary coach. Iba had coached gold-medal teams for the United States in the Olympics in 1964 and 1968 and then saw his Olympic team gypped in 1972 in Munich, when officials three times put time back on the clock after what appeared to be a one-point win over the Russian National team. On the third try, the Russians "won."

C. M. Newton, another legendary coach then at Vanderbilt, was the team manager for Knight. After everybody arrived in San Diego, where Knight's team was to scrimmage the next day with an NBA team in final preparation for the opening of the Olympic competition, I was about to grab a cab for my hotel, when C. M. insisted he would give me a ride because "there's something we need to talk about."

In the car, he told me, "You've got to talk to Knight. He wants to send Patrick Ewing home. And you're the only one at this point who can talk him into realizing we need this kid." Ewing, the 7-foot All-American center from Georgetown, who went on to stardom in the NBA with the New York Knicks, was expected to be a force under the basket for the United States in rebounding and shot-blocking as well as scoring. Sure, the team had other outstanding talent, including a player from North Carolina named Michael Jordan. But C. M. said the coaching staff was afraid that the loss of Ewing could leave the team vulnerable.

"Knight's furious with him," C. M. explained. Why? Because Ewing hurt his neck, pinched a nerve or something, and could hardly move his head. Well, it wasn't that he was hurt but rather the way he was hurt that had Bob so mad. Ewing and Jordan were roommates. They were clowning around, wrestling in their room, and Ewing was injured. Knight told his coaching staff he was so fed up that he was sending Ewing home.

The next morning, I was waiting at the bench in the gym where the team was practicing before the exhibition scrimmage. Knight came out and sat next to me, putting on his socks and sneakers as he launched into a denunciation of Ewing. "I can't believe how lazy he is," Knight is saying. "He doesn't work hard."

I'm just sitting there with my arms folded, saying: "Yeah, Bob, but you need him."

He's putting on his right shoe, lacing it up, and lacing into Ewing: "He doesn't show any enthusiasm."

"Yeah, Bob, but you need him."

He's putting on his left shoe, cursing out Ewing: "He's screwing around and gets hurt. Doesn't deserve to be on the team."

"Yeah, Bob, but you need him."

Knight, shoes tied, got up, walked away to direct the practice. As he left, however, he didn't repeat an intention of throwing Ewing off the team. I looked at C. M. Newton at the other end of the court and gave an OK sign. I didn't argue with Knight. That wouldn't have helped. I just kept telling him the truth. And I could tell he understood.

Ewing stayed on the team, recovered enough from the injury to show Knight the desired hustle, and blocked eighteen shots in the eight games that brought an Olympic gold medal. He also averaged eleven points and 5.6 rebounds a game as the team, led by Jordan, played the way Knight expected in demolishing every opponent.

The late Al McGuire also was like a brother to me. Al was head coach at Marquette for thirteen years, compiling a 78.7

winning percentage and capping his career with a national championship in 1977. He was a master of psychology. In contrast to Knight, Al wasn't a great strategist with Xs and Os. Nor did he carefully organize and orchestrate practices. He had superb assistants, Hank Raymonds and Rick Majerus, to handle the details. He concentrated more on the psychology of motivating, persuading, neutralizing, or rattling the crowds (home and away), the officials (good and bad), and the players (his and those on the other team).

Al might spend only the first fifteen minutes at a practice and then turn things over to the assistants. Sometimes during a game, as Al worked the officials and the crowd and motivated his players, his assistant, Raymonds, would turn to him with sage suggestions: "Why don't we go zone?" Al would signal "zone," and Marquette would put the clamps on the other team and go down to score. The TV guys would analyze: "What a great move by Al."

But Al would motivate his players in the huddle, get those kids playing all out. He was a showman who could rouse the crowd at home or get an away crowd to focus their attention on him rather than on distracting his players. He presented a striking figure, tall and with wavy hair, always a great dresser. He wore fashionable sports jackets, never a suit, and colorful ties. His glib speech and catchy sayings made him a natural for TV interviews and, after he quit coaching, for his role on basketball broadcasts.

He was a great recruiter, bringing to Marquette players from New York such as Dean "The Dream" Meminger. His charisma played a part in convincing high school stars that they wanted to play for him. And more than 92 percent of his Marquette players got their degrees. (Where are you, Jerry Tarkanian?)

My first experience with the McGuire psychology came when I was a rookie head coach at Fordham. We were good, playing well, and Al knew he was in for a tough game as halftime loomed. Al calls time-out and tells his son, Allie, a guard who was the playmaker for Marquette, to go over to the referee and "tell him he's a son of a bitch." Allie goes over to the official and delivers the message: "My dad says you're a son of a bitch." Al gets a technical foul. I'm thinking, "What was that all about?"

What it was about became clear later, in the last minute of the game. We're up two points and have the ball. Marquette knocks it out of bounds. It should be our ball. Al points toward his basket and looks at the referee. His players also point that it's their ball. The official, already aware from that first-half denunciation that McGuire thinks he's missing calls, is swayed by the pointing. Marquette ball. They tie the game. We lose in overtime.

There came another matchup after I learned some of this psychology with officials. My Notre Dame team that ended the UCLA streak at home in '74 then went out to Los Angeles and lost to UCLA there. Next we had a home game with Marquette. We're flat. We're down six or eight points. I call a time-out. Art White, a Big 10 official, walks toward the scorer's table. And Al, who knows I called the time-out but apparently wants to make sure I'm charged for it, yells, "Whose time-out?" I yell, "Television. It's a TV time-out." White signals a TV time-out, thus one not charged to Notre Dame. Al is furious. Gets a technical foul. I turn and look at him and say simply: "We're even for Fordham." He knows what I mean. We go on to win the game.

Soon, in our Marquette vs. Notre Dame games, as we each sought advantage in getting a technical foul at a strategic time to make a point with the officials, stir a crowd, motivate our players, or change momentum, there arose rumors of an unusual pool. Rumor had it that in the press room before our games the sports writers and broadcasters covering the Al and Digger show would each put a dollar in a pool to pick which of us would get the first technical and how many minutes it would be into the game. Just a rumor. Sure.

Rick Majerus, one of those fine assistants on whom Al relied at Marquette, told the *Milwaukee Journal Sentinel*, "Al almost didn't want to be labeled as a coach. He wanted his life to be more expansive rather than the one-dimensional box that most coaches have a tendency to put themselves into." He was his own man. Al one summer took his motorcycle and rode all around New Zealand. And when he won the national championship, beating

North Carolina in the NCAA title game, he retired from coaching at age forty-eight to do other things, including broadcasting.

Majerus, with fond reminiscences after Al's death in 2001, also told the Milwaukee paper that McGuire was the consummate competitor, whether it came to winning recruits or games or having someone else pick up the check for lunch. That was Al. He gave time and money to charities, but he enjoyed playing games over who would pick up the tab.

On a Thursday before a big Southern Cal football game at Notre Dame, Al called me to say he needed four tickets for the game. He was flying in from Milwaukee with three business types who wanted to see the game. "Are you crazy?" I blurted. "I don't have extra tickets. Why didn't you call me a week ago? Maybe I could have tracked down some tickets then. But now?"

Well, he knew I'd try. I went to see Roger Valdiserri, the Notre Dame sports information director. Roger loved Al. So did I. So did so many who knew him well. Al, in fact, had worked behind the scenes to convince Notre Dame to hire me as coach. Roger of course comes up with the tickets. Al arrives at the basketball office the Saturday morning of the game with his three buddies. They join us for some food. And as it's time to go to the stadium, Al comes in my back office, where I had the tickets.

"What do I owe you?" he asks.

"Nothing," I say. "Don't worry about it. You're our guests."

"Come on," he persists. "These guys got money. They can pay."

"No, I didn't pay for them," I explained. "I don't want money. You're guests of Notre Dame."

As he's going out the door, Al leans back and says, "I'm telling them you charged $150 apiece and collect $600." A month or so later, I'm talking to him on the phone. I asked, "Did you ever get that $600?"

"Yeah," he says, laughing. "I told them you were a son of a bitch and collected the money for yourself." I believe he really did that.

When I brought my Notre Dame teams to play UCLA in front of the boisterous crowd in Pauley Pavilion, I was Al

McGuire. I used his crowd psychology. With some McGuire-type showmanship I could get the crowd to focus on me, not my players, and also show the players that there was no reason to fear some hostile chants and derision. It was fun. And effective.

When Al died, I said that I had lost a brother. Indeed, I had.

Chapter 22

Digger as Artist and Van Gogh Freak

"As Shar realized, my painting did show a lot of turmoil. This was in 1990, when new Notre Dame administrators weren't supporting our basketball program in the way it had been by the people I revered, the people who hired me—Father Hesburgh, Father Joyce, and Moose Krause. The new administrators wanted their own coach. The handwriting was on the wall. And the turmoil was on the canvas in my painting. The 1990–91 season would be my last at Notre Dame."

Twenty-two

"Digger, have you done any painting lately?" That's a question I'm often asked by friends in South Bend. Those who know me only as a basketball coach or TV analyst probably assume such an inquiry would be about whether I painted some walls and ceilings in my house or maybe the garage door. I do painting, but not the kind involving a paint bucket and a ladder. I paint French vineyards, sunsets, hillsides, flowers, country scenes. Oils. Featuring bright colors.

Yep, Digger the artist. Some people like my paintings. Some buy them. Some hang them on their walls, right in their living rooms. I'm sure others have looked at my work and thought it would be wise for me instead to use a much larger brush and a paint bucket and slap colors on the walls rather than on a canvas. Not everybody has the same tastes in art. And frankly, I wouldn't care if nobody else liked my paintings. I love to paint.

To live life to the fullest, as I determined to do after becoming so familiar with the reality of death as an undertaker's son, I believe it's necessary to have a hobby, really to try more than one hobby or activity outside the normal daily routine. Sure, it can be tough to find the time. But try. It leads to more enjoyment of life and makes you more enjoyable to be around. Ever since I was a kid, I've collected stamps. Never, however, had I thought until toward the end of my coaching career at Notre Dame that I would ever paint a landscape.

My first serious interest in art and artists came right at the start of my Notre Dame coaching, when Terry and I went to

Europe for a vacation. It was my first trip to Europe. We visited museums in London, Amsterdam, and Paris and saw the works of the great artists.

I became a Van Gogh freak. His bright, vibrant colors and boldness appealed to me. And I was enthralled as I saw more of his paintings and learned about the great Dutch painter, the tragedies in his life, and his suicide in 1890 at age thirty-seven. Vincent Van Gogh, son of a minister, tried preaching but was dismissed by church authorities, who found him unsuited for the clergy. He was rejected by the woman he loved, and his family did not respect his work as an artist. In fact, there was not much respect anywhere for his paintings during his life. One can better understand the message in the paintings when the life and moods of the messenger are known.

My interest expanded to the work of other artists, especially that of the French painter Henri Matisse, leader of the Fauves (wild beasts), who were influenced by the post-Impressionists such as Van Gogh. Again, at the time, there was considerable scoffing at those in the Fauvist movement, who painted a tree trunk orange or some other bright color, if they chose, rather than a natural brown.

When I was on the NCAA committee on rules for basketball and on the board of the National Association of Basketball Coaches, I would sketch on a pad during meetings, something to do if a speaker was long-winded or the discussion was repetitive or trivial. Just a pad and a pencil. I did some other sketching just for fun.

Then, in 1990, I met LeRoy Neiman, the popular American artist, at a White House function. I told him of my great respect for his work, his brilliant colors in images of sporting events and leisure activities. As we talked, I mentioned my own interest in art and said I even enjoyed sketching.

"Sketching?" he said. "Why don't you try painting?"

"Well, I don't think I could do that," I told him.

"I think you should paint," he insisted. He asked me to send him some of my sketches. Send some of my stuff to LeRoy Neiman? Maybe he'd say: "You're right, Digger. Don't bother trying to paint."

When I got back home, I went to the studio of Shar Sosh, a highly acclaimed South Bend artist. She also encouraged me to try painting. She left me with a clear-glass vase with six yellow roses and told me to paint, not just paint six roses but to put on canvas something inspired by my thoughts as I contemplated.

It was my first painting. My love of bright colors was evident. There were four roses, with faces representing ugliness, happiness, sadness, and loneliness in what I titled *The Bloom of Four Faces*. I portrayed a tornado in one corner and a thunderstorm on the other side, both threatening, but with some blue sky, a room of solitude, and a sea of tranquility. A lot of emotions. A lot of oranges, yellows, and reds. A lot of painting that I never thought I would or could do.

"Wow!" Shar said. "Shows a lot of turmoil." She was very encouraging. It was kind of like the feeling I had when my scouting report and game plan enabled David (Rider) to beat Goliath (New York University) back in 1964. I thought: "I can do this."

As Shar realized, my painting did show a lot of turmoil. This was in 1990, when new Notre Dame administrators— Father Malloy, the president; Father Beauchamp, the executive vice president; and Richard Rosenthal, the athletic director— weren't supporting our basketball program in the way it had been by the people I revered, the people who hired me—Father Hesburgh, Father Joyce, and Moose Krause. The new administrators wanted their own coach. The handwriting was on the wall. And the turmoil was on the canvas in my painting. The 1990–91 season would be my last at Notre Dame.

I did send a few of my artistic efforts to Neiman, who insisted that he was right in encouraging me to paint, that I could and should do it. Anybody can paint. Really. I didn't think I could do it. Now, I know I can paint and enjoy it. You don't have to be a great painter. It's not a case of being either great or a flop. A lot of territory lies between those extremes. Paint a sky. Paint a sunset. If somebody thinks it's a painting of a soybean field, so be it. Try it. Try again. Or try some other new endeavor.

I paint mostly in the summer or fall. I'm too busy with ESPN and basketball in the other months. I've painted in France.

I've painted at my home in South Bend. I enjoy it. You transfer what you think, what you are, from mind to hand to canvas.

My love of Van Gogh once could have been costly. Very, very costly. While I may not remember correctly the exact numbers at an expensive art auction, I'll tell the story with what I recall as basically the amounts involved. The auction of a Van Gogh was happening in Chicago on the day after we played DePaul. Terry and I went. We were joined by Dr. Fred Ferlic, the team's orthopedic physician, and his wife, Mary. We heard that the painting had been purchased by a couple in a garage sale. The buyers, unaware of the painter's identity, had later asked an appraiser to look at another painting. The appraiser's attention turned instead to the bright colors and style of a different painting in their house, the one from the garage sale. "I think it could be a Van Gogh," the appraiser said after a close examination. It was. Experts authenticated it as one of the many Van Gogh paintings the artist did not sign.

We checked in as potential bidders and got our number and paddle to raise as the indication of a bid. Since I didn't think we had a chance of winning the masterpiece, I looked around, trying to guess the identity of the high bidder, probably some agent for the person who would be the real Van Gogh buyer. A man wearing a nice suit and a serious expression quietly came in alone as the auction was about to begin and took a seat in the second row. "That's the guy," I predicted.

Bidding began. It started at $100,000, as I recall. We got in on the early bidding as the auctioneer called for higher amounts—$200,000; $300,000; $400,000. "Come on, let's put up the paddle," I urged as the amount continued to climb. Fred was getting nervous. But I knew we'd get financing if we got a Van Gogh in this early bidding. We wouldn't win, I figured. Still, if we did, it would be almost as fortunate as getting that masterpiece in the garage sale. At about $700,000, we folded.

The guy in the suit in the second row still hadn't made a bid. There were people on telephone lines making bids along with a few in the audience as the price topped a million, topped two million. Finally, at about $2.4 million, the guy in the suit in the second row made his first bid. He got it at something like $2.8 million. While that was far beyond our bidding power, it still was a bargain. Just recently there was a newspaper story about a Van Gogh owned by a Chicago businessman fetching $40.3 million at an art auction in New York. And that was cheap compared to the $82.5 million paid for the great artist's *Portrait of Dr. Gachet* in 1990.

Oh, by the way, if you think you have spotted in some garage sale an unsigned masterpiece that I painted, don't buy it. Mine are all signed "Digger."

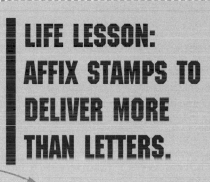

Chapter 23

One for the Gipper

"One of the toughest battles for me was winning approval for a Malcolm X stamp in 1999. Those streetwise young African Americans, Orlando and J. J., had convinced me during my Weed and Seed days in Washington to read the Malcolm X autobiography. And I had come away realizing that this charismatic black leader had turned to a message of nonviolence and brotherhood, rejecting the segregationist ideology of that time of the Nation of Islam. He sought the chance for blacks to make it in America in the same way that the Irish, the Polish, and the Italians had done in the past. Some who were reluctant to approve the stamp cited events and statements from earlier in Malcolm's life. But those of us who favored the stamp, including African Americans on the committee and around the nation, prevailed."

Twenty-three

When I started collecting stamps as a second-grader at South Avenue Grammar School in Beacon, never did I imagine in my wildest childhood dreams that it would lead to picking the themes for postage stamps and inviting a president of the United States to attend a ceremony for first-day sales of one of those stamps. But it did.

My stuck-on-stamps hobby began with fascination for features in the *Weekly Reader* on new issues of stamps. We talked about the *Reader* when it was distributed in school, as I guess kids did in schools in other parts of the country as well. I hope those stamp features led many others as well to a hobby adding to interest in life, enjoyment of life.

Fast-forward now from my second-grade class to coaching at Notre Dame. A stamp for the 1984 Summer Olympics to be held in Los Angeles was unveiled by the U.S. Postal Service during an Amateur Athletic Union basketball tournament hosted in 1983 by Notre Dame. I was invited for the ceremony. During the event, I mentioned to a postal official who was sitting next to me that I always had been interested in stamp collecting.

"Do you still collect?" he asked. When I told him yes and went on talking enthusiastically about my stamps and enjoyment of collecting, he had another question: "Why don't you consider being on the committee?"

"What committee?" I asked with some trepidation, thinking of how to politely decline service on one of those time-wasting committees. Probably this would be some group of windbags engaged in endless, inane discussions of how often to paint mailboxes or the wattage for lightbulbs in postal facilities. Instead, I heard about an important, exciting committee known as the Citizens' Stamp Advisory Committee. This fifteen-member committee appointed by the postmaster general considers all the proposals for subjects to appear on U.S. commemorative stamps and provides guidance on artwork and designs for the selected issues.

"I'd love to serve on that committee," I said. That December of '83, when an opening occurred on the committee, I was asked to serve, quickly accepted, and began what was initially to be a single twelve-year term. My service was extended for almost twice that long, until October of 2006. It was a rewarding experience.

We were the ones during that time picking the Christmas stamps; adding stamps for other holidays, including Hanukkah; and approving the series of "love" stamps. It was behind-the-scenes work. Few people know there is such a committee. I certainly didn't when it was first mentioned to me. The committee meets four times a year and follows strict guidelines in deciding on about twenty-five new subjects for commemorative stamps annually.

Never is there a lack of suggestions from organizations, institutions, and the general public. What a task it is to select from as many as fifty thousand recommendations each year for stamp subjects and designs. No living person can be honored by portrayal on a U.S. stamp, nor can a commemorative stamp for a person be issued sooner than five years after his or her death, with the exception of a deceased president, who can be honored with a memorial stamp on the first birth anniversary after death.

Only the president can order a particular stamp. Congress cannot. Sometimes powerful members of Congress seek to pressure the committee to select a subject of limited merit. The pressure doesn't work; if anything, it turns off the committee. Some requests, such as a stamp on the two hundredth anniversary of the founding of a university, are automatically approved.

As you can imagine, I was involved in advocating stamps in the areas of sports and social issues. Some of the biggest-selling stamps honored baseball. A highly successful sheet of stamps was issued in 2000 on legends of the game, portraying twenty great baseball players of the past, all Hall of Fame members. In the following year, we issued stamps with portrayals of famed major league playing fields, some still in use, such as Wrigley Field and Fenway Park, and others just memories for me and many long-time fans of the game, such as Ebbets Field and the New York Polo Grounds.

One of the toughest battles for me was winning approval for a Malcolm X stamp in 1999. Those streetwise young African Americans, Orlando and J. J., had convinced me during my Weed and Seed days in Washington to read the Malcolm X autobiography. And I had come away realizing that this charismatic black leader had turned to a message of nonviolence and brotherhood, rejecting the segregationist ideology of that time of the Nation of Islam. He sought the chance for blacks to make it in America in the same way that the Irish, the Polish, and the Italians had done in the past. Some who were reluctant to approve the stamp cited events and statements from earlier in Malcolm's life. But those of us who favored the stamp, including African Americans on the committee and around the nation, prevailed.

It is interesting that opposition to the stamp came also from a few who opposed the brotherhood message and quoted Elijah Muhammad, the Nation of Islam leader with whom Malcolm broke, as denouncing Malcolm's philosophy that "white people are good." Well, they are, most of them. So are black people, most of them. Malcolm understood that.

For a stamp ceremony very special to me, I went to the White House to extend an invitation for the president to attend. The stamp, issued in March of 1988, honored legendary Notre Dame football coach Knute Rockne on the hundredth anniversary of his birth. The invitation was to President Ronald Reagan, who in his Hollywood career appeared in the 1940 movie *Knute Rockne—All American*. Reagan was "the Gipper" in the motion picture, playing the part of George Gipp, Rockne's star halfback.

Whether Reagan would attend was far from certain. Presidents don't often make more than one appearance at any university during their time in the White House. Reagan had delivered the commencement address at Notre Dame in May of 1981, making his first public appearance after the attempt on his life.

But Reagan accepted. On March 9, 1988, he delivered a nostalgic address, telling how the George Gipp role was "a young actor's dream" and praising what Rockne meant to football and Notre Dame. He closed with a message to students that there will be tough days as well as joy and triumph. With a paraphrase from the famed movie scene in which Gipp, on his deathbed, talks with Rockne about inspiring the team to victory on some future day, Reagan said:

"There will also be times of despair. Times when all of those around you are ready to give up. It is then I want you to remember our meeting today and 'some time when the team is up against it and the breaks are beating the boys, tell them to go out there with all they've got and win just one for the Gipper. I don't know where I'll be then, but I'll know about it, and I'll be happy.'"

There was thunderous applause in the packed Athletic and Convocation Center. And tears in some eyes as well, as "the Gipper," in the final year of his presidency, said goodbye. President Reagan, still with an actor's knowledge of what makes a good scene, also picked up a football and tossed a prearranged "touchdown pass" to Tim Brown, Notre Dame's Heisman Trophy winner.

Postmaster General Anthony M. Frank, who had just assumed that post at the start of the month, was ecstatic about the ceremony for the Rockne stamp. "Boy, are all the first-day ceremonies like this?" the postmaster wondered.

"No," I told him. "The president doesn't show up, and there aren't twelve thousand people."

A very different response to a first-day issue of a new stamp was experienced by Frank early in 1991, when he unveiled a stamp commemorating the hundredth anniversary of basketball during halftime in our exhibition game with the Soviet National Team in Springfield, Massachusetts. That's the city where James

Naismith invented the game with use of a soccer ball and peach baskets. The fans in Springfield booed the postmaster general. Why? The price of a first-class stamp had just gone up from twenty-five cents to twenty-nine cents. "Hey, Tony," I said. "Little bit different than at Notre Dame." We laughed. He was a good postmaster general. And he wasn't the one to set the postal rates.

Membership on the stamp committee is diverse, with people selected from many fields, most of them highly successful and all with an interest in picking appropriate and popular subjects for our postage. One of the most impressive people I met on the stamp committee was Karl Malden, the Oscar-winning actor whose remarkable career in films, on stage, and in television spanned more than six decades. He worked at his craft tirelessly. Once in talking about his role in the movie *Patton*, in which he played Gen. Omar Bradley, Karl told of how he went to see the general to ask for advice on how to present an accurate portrayal. He thought Bradley no doubt showed real anger in one encounter with Gen. George S. Patton. "Bradley said he wasn't angry, just very concerned," Malden said. "So that's how I played the scene."

Many people also remember Malden's TV commercials for American Express and his advice: "Don't leave home without it." When Karl was in his nineties, we had a dinner in Los Angeles honoring him. After all the accolades, Karl got up to respond. We were there to honor him and thank him for all he had done, and now he was thanking us, closing with a statement that also was a powerful reminder.

"Thanks for making me feel needed," he said.

For me and I'm sure for others at the dinner, this was a reminder that even a man of such achievements, a man with such a long and successful life, still appreciated knowing he was remembered, not forgotten; important to us, not brushed aside; looked to yet for his wisdom, not looked upon as no longer offering anything of value.

"Thanks for making me feel needed."

Unlike some other cultures where the experience and wisdom of age is honored, we too often make our senior citizens feel

unneeded, that they are burdens. Tough it was making the decisions on honorees on commemorative stamps. For most of us,
however, it would not be tough at all to honor some of the
people who had a great influence in our lives. Unlike the rule on
stamps, we don't have to wait until after their deaths.

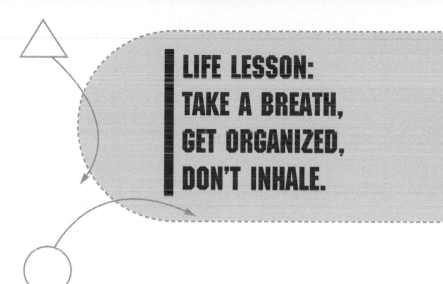

LIFE LESSON: TAKE A BREATH, GET ORGANIZED, DON'T INHALE.

Chapter 24

Relax: Stress Is Stressful

"Relax for a minute. Get organized. Find the customer order in the briefcase before calling the boss. You'll sound a lot more professional. Find the information on the computer before calling the customer. You'll sound a lot more persuasive. Put aside the work for just a bit to sip instead of gulp the coffee and chew rather than inhale the sweet roll. Better yet, get organized earlier in order to have a more nutritious breakfast. You'll lower risks of such little annoyances as an ulcer or a heart attack."

Twenty-four

Since I spend a lot of time in airports, what with travel for ESPN, trips for celebrity golf tournaments and other appearances, and for visits with family and friends, I have an opportunity to observe other airline passengers. And worry about them.

One worry is if some guy fitting what we think of as the terrorist profile is acting in a strange or nervous way. Sometimes I've sought to strike up a conversation with such a person, usually finding responses that alleviated my concern. Sure, all who fit a profile aren't terrorists, and all who are terrorists don't fit a profile. But why not be cautious?

Another worry is over stress that is so apparent in so many fellow passengers as they frantically juggle carry-ons, BlackBerries, computers, cell phones, tickets, boarding passes, newspapers, books, or snacks, or maybe all of that in the rush to the departure area, often out of breath. Soon they may also be out of patience as they find that their flight has been delayed or cancelled.

The health of our population is a worry. Too much obesity. Still too much smoking. Far too much tension. One early morning at the airport in Pittsburgh, I saw Mr. Ultimate Stress. He and I were waiting for a flight. And I couldn't help but notice the nervous, fidgeting Mr. Stress as he sought to talk on his cell phone, operate his laptop computer, find papers in his briefcase, drink a large coffee, and eat a sugary sweet roll that probably was his alternative to a healthy breakfast.

Why? Relax for a minute. Get organized. Find the customer order in the briefcase before calling the boss. You'll sound a lot more professional. Find the information on the computer before calling the customer. You'll sound a lot more persuasive. Put aside the work for just a bit to sip instead of gulp the coffee and chew rather than inhale the sweet roll. Better yet, get organized earlier in order to have a more nutritious breakfast. You'll lower risks of such little annoyances as an ulcer or a heart attack.

Even when I'm at the Hartford airport by 5:00 a.m. to catch a six o'clock flight in heading back to South Bend, I hear strangers babbling away on cell phones. To whom are they talking at that hour? Maybe it's somebody in Europe or Asia. Sure can't be somebody on the West Coast at the hour it is out there.

As an undertaker's son, I saw the stress faced by the family of the deceased and the stress my father felt in trying to make sure everything was just right at the wake, the service, and the burial. As a college coach, stress was a constant companion in dealing with game pressure, the whims of young athletes, the attitudes of referees, the expectations of fans at home, the effects on the team of jeering fans at away games, and the questioning of the sports writers and commentators.

One of the ways for me to relieve stress is listening to music. You don't have to set aside a whole evening to go to a concert or to the opera or to listen for hours to favorite albums—although that's nice when you have the time. Just mellow out for a few minutes. Put aside problems and pressures for at least a brief interlude of listening to and enjoying the music you like. If you can, let the music play on as you return to whatever it is that you must do. Problems often seem easier to solve with a little musical background. Ailments, from headaches to stress-induced stomach woes, often seem to disappear while you listen to music. Doctors probably could help more people by replacing that "take two aspirins" routine with new advice: "Listen to two songs, and call me in the morning."

In addition to helping you to mellow out, music can motivate, inspire. I used music in the locker room before games to get players in the right mood as they took the court. For his successful 1992 presidential race, Bill Clinton used "Don't Stop (Thinking about Tomorrow)" by Fleetwood Mac as a campaign theme song. Just the right tempo. Just the right words. For a 2008 campaign theme song, a great choice would be "Why Can't We Live Together" by Sade or, maybe even better, "Brand New Day" by Sting.

Music is like pizza. Just about everybody enjoys both. But tastes vary. There are all kinds of options. For pizza, the choices include pepperoni, anchovies, olives, mushrooms, sausage, and pineapple, with deep-dish or thin crust as added options. For music, the choices include opera, jazz, hip-hop, Broadway, rap, and pop vocals, with added options of volume and video.

I've compiled a list of my twenty favorites. Not everybody will like them all. You may scoff at the entire list. That's okay. Maybe I wouldn't like what you order on your pizza or your music selections. But that shouldn't keep us from enjoying our own pizza choices, our own music selections. Make your own list of music. And why not at least give a listen to some of the music on my list?

Digger's Top 20 Songs and Their Albums

1. Barry White, "Love Unlimited" in *Love Unlimited*

2. Grover Washington Jr., "East Side Drive" in *Anthology*

3. Marc Antoine, "Cruisin'" in *Cruisin'*

4. Chris Botti, "Midnight without You" in *Midnight without You*

5. Moby, "Porcelain" in *Play*

6. The Rolling Stones, "You Can't Always Get What You Want" in *Let It Bleed*

7. Rick Braun, *Esperanto*

8. The Urban Grooves, "Long Way from Brooklyn" in *Down to the Bone*

9. Sting, "Brand New Day" in *Brand New Day*

10. Phil Collins, "Sussudio" in *No Jacket Required*

11. Steve Winwood, "My Love's Leavin'" in *Back in the High Life*

Out to dinner in the late 1940s after seeing the play *Oklahoma*—Digger, his paternal grandmother, his father, and his mother (*from left to right*). (Courtesy Digger Phelps)

Digger with sister Diane (*left*), his mother (*back right*), and sister Barbara (*front right*) in 1951. (Courtesy Digger Phelps)

The 1954 Police Athletic League summer baseball team—Digger is fourth from left in back row wearing a cap. (Courtesy Digger Phelps)

Digger and his parents during the 1970s in front of his childhood home at 13 Cottage Place in Beacon, New York. (Courtesy Digger Phelps)

Digger with fellow coach and friend Al McGuire in the 1970s.
(Courtesy Digger Phelps)

Digger roams the
sidelines during an
NCAA tournament
game in the late 1980s.
(Simon C. Griffiths)

Digger barks out instructions during a game against Louisville in Indianapolis during the 1987–88 season. (Cheryl A. Ertelt)

Toe-to-toe with Special Olympics coach Butch Waxman, the only coach to go undefeated against Digger at 33-0. (International Summer Special Olympic Games / Courtesy Digger Phelps)

Digger with his artistic mentor, LeRoy Neiman. (Neal P. Kemp)

Another source of inspiration: Digger with his spiritual guide, Notre Dame's Rev. Theodore M. Hesburgh. (Courtesy Digger Phelps)

The birth of democracy in Cambodia: the first woman to vote at Digger's polling station in May 1993. (Courtesy Digger Phelps)

Digger (*at right*) aboard Air Force One with President George H. W. Bush and advisers discussing the Weed and Seed program. (Courtesy Digger Phelps)

Setting up a play in a typical timeout scene with the Fighting Irish.
(Dlugolecki Photography)

Digger with Muhammad Ali in 1997 at The Greatest's home in
Berrien Springs, Michigan. (Courtesy Digger Phelps)

Digger speaks at a Notre Dame pep rally before the 2006 UCLA football game. (Mike Bennett/Lighthouse Imaging)

12. Ramsey Lewis, "Watermelon Man" in *Wade in the Water*

13. Carlos Santana, "Smooth" in *Supernatural*

14. Tina Turner, "Whatever You Want" in *Wildest Dreams*

15. Keiko Matsui, "Whisper from the Mirror" in *Whisper from the Mirror*

16. Sheryl Crow, "Run, Baby, Run" in *Tuesday Night Music Club*

17. Elton John, "Simple Life" in *The One*

18. Jazz Crusaders, "Clima Suave" in *Soul Axess*

19. Fiona Apple, "A Mistake" in *When the Pawn . . .*

20. Praful, "Sigh" in *One Day Deep*

Don't underestimate the value of humor in dealing with stress.

Even the pressure of being on ESPN, with a producer talking in your ear about how little time is left and knowledge that a flub goes nationwide, listening to the funny quips of a broadcast partner like Dick Vitale can turn a stressful situation into a pleasure.

The jokes and pranks of my mother helped to relieve stress in our family when business wasn't good or her son was having problems with Latin. Just thinking back to some of the funny escapades with my friend Caesar can bring a smile to replace a frown of concern.

A frustrating situation can be coped with much better if you see some humor in the circumstances. For example, I was in a coffee place early one morning in Washington during my Weed and Seed days when I was beeped with a message to call the White House; the president wanted to talk with me. I needed a landline rather than my cell phone, and I asked a young lady working in the place if I could use their phone. She kindly agreed to let me use a phone right by the counter.

So I'm talking to the president of the United States about an upcoming presidential debate and key points he could make about our Weed and Seed effort and about supporting material that I would get immediately to the White House.

As I'm conversing with the president for three minutes, maybe five, people are coming in for their bagels and coffee. I'm right by where the young lady is at the cash register, taking orders. Frustrating? Well, it would probably have been easier to be at my desk and not have chatter about café mocha orders, everything bagels, and the special coffee blend going on so close by as I tried to hear all that the president was saying. Instead, since really I could hear his voice quite well, stress of the situation was replaced by a realization of the humor of the situation. The sleepy customers eager for their coffee had no idea this guy jabbering on the phone was talking with President Bush.

The young lady, however, put two and two together, probably through hearing me say "Mr. President" and hearing some of the substance of the conversation. She was looking in amazement when I hung up, thanked her, and confirmed it was a call to the president. She'll probably tell her grandchildren about it someday. And I left with a smile, not a frown, over having to make the call from what could have been a frustrating location.

Down in the dumps? Think of something funny. In a frustrating situation? Think of the humor that could be found in the circumstances. Lost a loved one? Mourn, sure, but also think of fun times, funny times with that loved one. Under stress? Call a friend who is known for a sense of humor. Or, if it's during basketball season, tune in Dick Vitale.

As we consider how to relieve stress, there is another consideration. Do we cause stress in others? Sure, we all do at times. Usually unintentionally. But intentional or not, we can do our part in avoiding some of the things that bug others. I also have a list for that, a list of the twelve things that bug me. Not all big things. Still, annoying things that no doubt disturb other folks as well. Here's my list:

Digger's Dozen Downers

1. Walking on a sidewalk or in a shopping mall and having people who refuse to stay to the right bumping into you or forcing you into the gutter or into the side of a store.

2. Stopping at a traffic light or four-way stop and then, when it's your turn to go, finding some yahoo shooting through the intersection to usurp the right-of-way and risk a collision.

3. Leaving safe space between your car and the vehicle in front of you on an interstate, only to have some jerk zoom around you and into the space.

4. Getting interrupted by someone who jumps into a conversation or discussion when you're right in the middle of telling a story.

5. Having someone try to finish your thought or interject a premature answer, especially when, as so often happens, they are wrong.

6. Pushing option after option in response to a business telephone-answering message without getting the option you need or finding how to reach a human being who could answer your inquiry.

7. Standing in a long line at a bank, postal facility, or similar enterprise when only a couple windows are open and ten other people behind closed windows putter around with other work deemed more important than customer service.

8. Sitting on an aisle seat on a plane and getting whacked on the shoulder, the knee, or the head by careless passengers meandering down the aisle with their bulky carry-ons, computers, and packages.

9. Failing to find items viewed, used, or borrowed by a guest or visitor who neglected to put the items back in their proper place in my house, where I keep and want everything just so.

10. Hearing the moaning of people who put off paying their bills until a first-of-the-month deadline, when most of them, with careful budgeting, could have paid the bills, as I do, when they arrive.

11. Blabbering incessantly and loudly on a cell phone by some loudmouth sitting next to you on a plane, at a game, or even at the theater.

12. Parading in public by teens who make an ugly appearance as they mistakenly think they are cute or cool, such as obese girls exposing fat stomachs and thighs in revealing dress and creepy boys tripping over low-slung pants as they expose unsightly abs and underwear.

That's just me. You may have your own list of pet peeves. More important than your list or mine is whether you or I do things that bug others, leading to even more stress in our society.

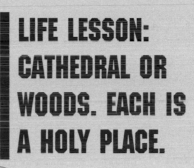

Chapter 25

Hesburgh Asks: "What Have You Really Been Doing?"

"Father Hesburgh has inspired many people to strive for worthy goals and in many cases achieve them. He inspires through words and deeds. His priestly concern for my welfare and desire that I strive for goals beyond a good golf score inspired me to dedicate time and energy to do what I could to improve the plight of kids in our troubled schools. While I had interest in promoting mentoring and after-school programs to get kids off the streets during the times they so often get into trouble, I then became determined to do more, to get out front in my own community and speak out wherever I could."

Twenty-five

My spiritual beliefs include living life to the fullest, not just for fun, fame, or fortune, all of which are nice, but to help others along the way and to try to make the world a little better. That I tried to do with Operation Weed and Seed. And in coaching, too, where I sought victories but also graduation for my players and doing things the right way for the honor of Notre Dame. God didn't give us this time to waste. Nor should we race on without ever thinking about the purpose of life.

There are three special, holy places for me, places where I can reflect on this philosophy, meditate, pray, and feel spiritual renewal. One is the Grotto at Notre Dame. I love the Grotto, a famous campus site. The outdoor, stone shrine to Mary, the mother of Jesus, is patterned after the original Grotto of Our Lady at Lourdes in France. It is a place for quiet contemplation and prayer, visited not only by Catholics but also by folks of other faiths as well. Candles can be lit for special intentions.

I have a rack of five candles that I light, each with a prayer for a family member or maybe a friend who is ill or sometimes for people who never dreamed that Digger was saying a prayer for them. That spot before the candles I light, affording my favorite view of the statue of Mary, is of special significance to me. Not that I'm superstitious, but if anybody's in my spot, I kick 'em out. I tell 'em that's my spot, guaranteed in the buyout of my coaching contract. They understand the point, if not the humor.

When I'm out of town and run into somebody who is facing some medical, personal, or career problem, I'll say, "When I get back, I'll light a candle for you at the Grotto." Occasionally, I get a quizzical look. Not everybody has heard of the Grotto. So I explain that it means really, "I'll say a prayer for you."

While the Grotto is my favorite campus site for quiet contemplation, the beautiful Sacred Heart Basilica is the setting for very special services that I try never to miss on Holy Thursday and Good Friday, Holy Week days before Easter. Midnight Mass at Christmas is magnificent. Nothing against the Vatican, but Notre Dame holds its own on those special days of spirituality.

A second place that brings special spiritual satisfaction is St. Patrick's Cathedral in New York City. Again, I have my own place, a spot in what is called the Lady Chapel, a section for devotion to Our Lady, Mary, mother of Jesus. My seat is in a particular row, first seat on the aisle, next to the second pillar, on the left side facing Mary.

St. Patrick's is an impressive Gothic structure right in the middle of New York City, a place of calm amid the bustle. The late Cardinal Spellman once said of the church in a sermon: "At its portals, the world seems left behind, and every advancing step brings Heaven nearer and deepens the soul's union with Divinity."

The third place very special to me in a spiritual sense is a chapel that is minute in comparison with the great cathedral in New York. This little chapel with only about seventy seats is back in my home Beacon area. It is operated by the Capuchin Franciscans, a religious order of brothers and priests inspired by the life and ideals of St. Francis of Assisi. When I'm back in Beacon, I stop there to light candles—top left of the cluster—and pause to pray and reflect in the second seat on the left-hand side. Maybe I seek out seating and candles on the left in these holy places because I'm left-handed. I'm not sure. I just know where I feel most at home, at peace, and in touch with things spiritual.

Memories abound at the Capuchins' chapel:

— Memories of childhood, of Mass when it was all in
   Latin. A book called a missal provided the translation,
   vital for somebody like me. Then and later, when it

took five tries to pass Latin in high school, that language was "Greek" to me. The service was impressive. So was the unwavering faith of my mother.

— Memories of returning through the years, including once in the mid-1980s, at the height of coaching success at Notre Dame, when Terry and I and the kids returned to Beacon for Christmas. There at midnight Mass in a nearby row was a lady I remembered from high school days. I wanted to date her, had a crush on her back then. But she would never go out with me. Well, Terry was wearing a mink coat. And as we walked down the aisle to Communion, I noticed the lady looking at the mink coat. I leaned over and said softly, "Coulda been yours." Spiritual moment? Perhaps not. But it was fun.

I take walks around the lakes at Notre Dame. Just walk all around the campus, sometimes to the priests' cemetery, maybe to visit the Basilica, always to view the famed Golden Dome with the statute of the Virgin Mary atop it. I think back to what it must have been like back in 1842, when Father Edward Sorin, a young priest of the Congregation of Holy Cross, a French missionary order, and seven Holy Cross brothers founded the school in what then was wilderness. Notre Dame to me is sacred ground.

Especially powerful is the "hidden crucifix" in the woods just off of Moreau Drive. The cross is on a mound in the midst of the woods, with a statue of Mary, the mother of Jesus, on the right side and a statue of Mary Magdalene on the left. This place of solitude, away from routes of tourists, football fans, and students, is to me the most sacred ground on Notre Dame's campus in times of a crisis.

Now, don't get the impression I'm staking claim to a saintly life. By no means. Anyone who knows me would brand such a claim as preposterous. But all of us, sinners though all of us are at times, whether few times or many times, need a spiritual uplift. For me, the uplift is not in going to Mass every Sunday—or every day, as my mother did. That's what she felt spiritually, what she

needed. For me, it's those more private moments that are significant, at the Grotto, at St. Patrick's, at the Capuchin chapel or
walking, contemplating on campus.

Homilies at Mass sometimes cause me to shake my head.
The sermons just aren't about the world out there with which we
must cope. They don't provide spiritual guidance or uplift. I'm
disturbed even more, of course, by the terrible scandals of priests
molesting children and then someone in authority such as the
disgraced Cardinal Law in Boston ignoring the situation. Since I
grew up with such respect for priests, it is difficult for me to
understand the betrayal. It angers me that these creeps in collars
have diminished the public perception of all our clergy. This no
doubt is a factor in the shortage of young men today who want to
become priests. Not as many mothers hope, as mine did, that a
son will become a priest. The shortage is a serious problem in
many parishes, with no priest in some cases to celebrate Mass or
take care of the needs of the faithful.

The problem could be resolved if priests again were allowed
to marry, as was permitted back in church history for priests and
popes. The problem of sex abuse by priests also could have been
alleviated if there still were married priests. And the homilies on
the subject of marriage and family would be more meaningful if
spoken by a priest who understood more about the subject.

Another solution would be ordination of women as priests.
Why not? Many in the clergy, including some I most respect,
would welcome this change, although they may refrain from
open advocacy because of fear of Vatican sanctions. The argument that Jesus had only males as apostles at the Last Supper is
to me and to many other Catholics a weak argument for allowing
only men to be priests.

Did the authors of the Gospels in years after the event
really include every detail, every participant? We know many
accounts are sketchy. Wouldn't Jesus, knowing this would be his
last supper, want his mother there? Since he clearly had women
as well as men among his followers and showed disdain for the
sexism of the day, isn't it possible that Mary Magdalene was
there?

Mary Magdalene was at the crucifixion. She was there on Easter morning. Then, despite her central role, she was brushed aside for centuries by the male theologians and clergy as supposedly just a loose woman, even as a prostitute, from whom Jesus cast seven devils. Her reputation today is restored to a point where she is even a pop heroine as well as an inspiration to women who seek a greater role in the Church.

Dan Brown's best-selling book, *The Da Vinci Code*, fictionalizes a sensational role for Mary Magdalene as married to Jesus and giving birth to start a royal but secret bloodline. This is fiction. A novel, not gospel. Brown does not claim otherwise. But would it be sheer fantasy to suggest, as the novel does, that perhaps Mary Magdalene was at the Last Supper? Perhaps through some type of fantasy you get a reality.

As coach at Notre Dame, I required my players to attend the team Mass before each game. By no means were they all Catholics. I never sought to convert anyone. I never required acceptance of any doctrine. And attending was never an issue. They all knew they were attending a Catholic university where they would encounter symbols and practices of the church. We didn't pray at Mass that we would win the game. There are more important things to ask of God than winning a basketball game. We prayed that we would play well and represent our team and university well.

We had only one proclaimed atheist. I just told him to sit in the back during Mass and meditate. I didn't expect him to fake prayer. But I'm sure atheists meditate and contemplate and think about right and wrong. While I sought no conversion there either, I don't believe he is an atheist today.

Players took turns with readings during Mass. They could regard them as from sacred Scripture or just as historical accounts. The purpose was twofold. It provided an opportunity for players who were mentally and physically prepared to dwell at least briefly on the spiritual. The second reason was that I wanted them to be prepared also to speak in public. Many kids entering college as freshmen have never spoken in front of a crowd and fear even speaking up in a classroom. We would start at the first

Masses with senior players and senior managers doing the readings and then work down to the freshmen as the season progressed. If a kid stumbled over a word, nobody snickered. As they learned to pronounce smoothly the biblical sites and names in the readings, they gained confidence.

This is one of the reasons we received much praise for the poised manner in which the senior players spoke at our basketball banquet. No stumbling and mumbling, no desecration of the English language and embarrassment of the type we suffer through when some athletes are interviewed on television. Also of help, of course, was that we recruited smart kids who studied and went to class.

Father Hesburgh is the person who inspired me spiritually more than anyone else. The word "great" is overused. Not, however, in the case of Hesburgh, a great man who led Notre Dame as its president, from 1952 to 1987, and achieved national acclaim and international respect in religion, education, and government. He served presidents and popes and was a leading advocate for civil rights and for ending nuclear-weapons testing.

He also has been a friend, always supportive and encouraging when I was coaching and he was president. He wanted successful athletic teams, but never at the expense of the academic excellence that Father Ted brought to Notre Dame. He has remained concerned about my welfare and continues to be an inspiration. To me, Father Hesburgh is as a priest as Mother Teresa was as a nun. Remarkable. And great. He is caring, loving, and has a way to challenge you to give back to the have-nots, to make a positive difference in confronting negative influences in the world.

In 1996, when we met at a Notre Dame function, Hesburgh asked me, "So what have you been doing?" I told him about my job as a basketball analyst for ESPN, a pretty good deal, with all summer off to play golf and travel.

"No, what have you really been doing?" he asked. Hesburgh wanted to know spiritually, for the soul, what was I doing to follow the philosophy that he and I share that one should try to make the world a little better, to do some good along the way.

We had talked before about the educational crisis in the secondary schools in this country. I was well aware of it, both in seeing some of those schools in recruiting players and then in directing Weed and Seed in troubled areas in America.

Father Hesburgh has inspired many people to strive for worthy goals and in many cases achieve them. He inspires through words and deeds. His priestly concern for my welfare and desire that I strive for goals beyond a good golf score inspired me to dedicate time and energy to do what I could to improve the plight of kids in our troubled schools. While I had interest in promoting mentoring and after-school programs to get kids off the streets during the times they so often get into trouble, I then became determined to do more, to get out front in my own community and speak out wherever I could.

I am afraid of death, as most people are. But less so now, thanks to Father Hesburgh and his inspiration for doing more for schools, for kids. There can be no better preparation for death than doing the best you can in living life.

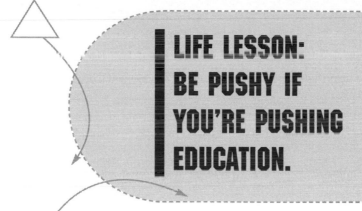

Chapter 26

Giving Volume to Small Voices

"We sought to raise $175,000. We hit $200,000. As I challenged others to contribute, I put my money where my mouth was with my own $5,000 for the project. There were contributions of supplies and equipment by businesses, including $20,000 worth of paint and brushes from Sherwin Williams. Food was donated to feed the volunteers during their workday. But most important were the hours donated by the volunteers, including families from the Lincoln neighborhood."

Twenty-six

Inspired by Father Hesburgh to do more, especially in seeking to remedy the inadequacy of our schools and, thus, to help the kids who fall through the cracks, I decided to start right at home, in South Bend. But how?

The South Bend school system, like so many, has budget problems. There isn't the money to provide all the after-school programs that could keep kids from wandering the streets from 3:00 to 5:00 p.m., those hours that statistics show to be danger times of temptation and getting into trouble. Nor is there always the funding to fix up, brighten up some of the older schools in less-affluent neighborhoods. Kids need to have pride in their school, not regard it as a dump where they are dumped by an uncaring educational system.

Borrowing from two successful programs with which I was familiar, I became determined to promote an effort to fix up an older school in an area where a large percentage of the students are from families in the poverty range. One program that provided the concept of volunteers working together to help the poor and improve the community was Habitat for Humanity. This international effort to provide decent, affordable shelter for the poor, through construction of new homes or renovation of older structures, has become well known through the efforts of former President Jimmy Carter. In addition to helping to publicize the effort, Carter joins once a year in picking up hammer and saw and participating in the carpentery work in a selected project area. If a former president could join in the actual physical labor, I figured I could require anybody who came to our school project, including the congressman and civic leaders, to pitch in and not just show up to make a pitch for the TV cameras.

A second program that provided some ideas for a school fix-up was called Christmas in April, a highly successful spring project in South Bend that involved volunteers, hundreds of them Notre Dame and Saint Mary's College students, swarming into a chosen neighborhood to fix up houses, with materials and expertise provided by the business community and union building trades members. Why couldn't we get donations of paint and other materials for our schools? Why couldn't we get folks with construction expertise to supervise our volunteers? We could. We did.

In a speech to the South Bend Rotary Club, the city's leading service club, I challenged the members to take on the project of fixing up a local school. The club, known for its good works, was seeking a project at that time and accepted my challenge. The club would be the sponsoring organization for what we dubbed "The 3 Rs of Summertime," referring to our goal of providing a "refreshed, renovated, and renewed" school when classes resumed in the fall.

Lincoln Elementary School, on the city's southeast side, was selected for the project. It was picked because it was built in 1910 and needed renovation that wasn't on the school administration's list for future repair for at least a decade. It served more than six hundred children, many from families below the poverty line. It was just what we were looking for, and Lincoln principal Edward Bradford Jr. enthusiastically embraced the concept, hailing community involvement in what he believed to be "a very positive manner." Virginia Calvin, the school superintendent, also welcomed the effort.

We sought to raise $175,000. We hit $200,000. As I challenged others to contribute, I put my money where my mouth was with my own $5,000 for the project. There were contributions of supplies and equipment by businesses, including $20,000 worth of paint and brushes from Sherwin Williams. Food was donated to feed the volunteers during their workday. But most important were the hours donated by the volunteers, including families from the Lincoln neighborhood.

Never have I been more proud of anything with which I've been involved. Beating those No. 1–rated basketball teams was great, and I'm proud of our success at Notre Dame. But this was a more important game, helping some kids beat the odds in the game of life.

On June 20, 1998, a Saturday, more than seven hundred people showed up at Lincoln to paint walls, wash woodwork, rip out old carpet and blackboards, and prepare to affix replacements, install new ceiling tiles and lighting fixtures, polish railings, plant flowers and shrubbery, trim trees, and plan for after-school projects. Most of the work was done on that one frantic day, for which the sponsoring Rotarians had joined in organizing well, with specific instructions for paint colors for each room and with color-coded T-shirts for the crowd: yellow for security, black for leaders, aqua for Rotary members, white for school families, royal blue for skilled tradespeople, red for nurses.

Work would go on later with reinstalling windows and completing new dropped ceilings and installation of new lighting and the all-important provision for after-school activities that were a key part of the project.

We drew national attention. NBC's *The Today Show* ran a live early-morning report. ESPN sent a camera crew. Local news coverage in the newspaper, on television, and on radio was extensive. The coverage was important. To me, this was a pilot project to be promoted for use elsewhere. My hope was then, and is now, that similar projects would be sponsored by Rotary Clubs in other communities around the nation or by other sponsoring organizations. If we are to save our schools, this type of involvement by the community, with strong commitment from the business sector, is necessary.

A brighter school offering after-school programs would be of no real value if it didn't get a positive response from the kids. The principal and teachers reported that the kids took pride in the spruced-up Lincoln. More than three hundred began attending the after-school programs that included a stamp club, art and music opportunities, creative writing, and a cooking class that was the most popular of all. Food was important for a lot of these kids, ones who have experienced hunger.

Rotary has done summer projects at other South Bend schools as well since then. But Lincoln was the start, the outstanding example of what can be built up in a school and a neighborhood through community involvement.

Then a school superintendent announced plans to tear down all that we built up. I was shocked when I saw a news story in the April 27, 2004, *South Bend Tribune* with the headline RAYMOND WANTS LINCOLN SCHOOL CLOSED BY 2006. "Raymond" is Joan Raymond, who by then had become the school superintendent. She told the school board that Lincoln, which had become a primary center—kindergarten through the fourth grade—with three hundred students, should be closed. Abandoned. She said it was the oldest school building in the system and closing it could save money at a time of projected budget shortfall.

Worst of all, she suggested as "food for thought" that the Lincoln kids could be sent off to another school far to the south, no doubt involving more busing and hurting the Lincoln neighborhood. What would happen to the after-school programs that had developed at Lincoln, with two-thirds of the kids participating in at least one of the activities? What would happen to the kids? To the neighborhood? Did Raymond care?

At the next school-board meeting, I was there to ask those and other questions. An old school? Sure. But many an old building is more substantial than structures built today. The Golden Dome is old. But Notre Dame doesn't tear it down. It's repaired when needed in a timely fashion.

Raymond and some board members who supported her on dooming Lincoln were far from thrilled to see me at that and other board meetings I attended. They knew that I could attract news-media attention and carry the fight for Lincoln to the public. The Lincoln kids had no voice in this. Nor did the Lincoln parents and neighborhood residents, most of whom would have felt intimidated by the superintendent and board if they had gone to a public meeting. Didn't bother me. Heck, it wasn't anything like facing all those Kentucky fans in Freedom Hall in Louisville as they welcomed me as a visiting coach.

Raymond and some of the board members turned to statistics that I did not believe. She claimed it would cost some $13 million to renovate Lincoln in order to keep it open. Some board members grew skeptical as well. This was going to be a battle, in my view a battle for the Lincoln kids and the retention of a neighborhood school that was doing a great job.

Also concerned about the fate of Lincoln was Gayle Dantzler, editorial page editor of the *South Bend Tribune*. She allowed space for an op-ed piece in which I presented the case for saving Lincoln. I noted that the huge cost estimate by Raymond for renovation included roof replacement and disclosed that I had asked a local roof contractor to examine the school. "He estimated that the roof needs about $10,000 worth of patching now and another $10,000 to give the roof five to ten years of additional life. He didn't charge a fee for this observation," I wrote, "but I see in the [Raymond] overview that $1,653,600 is listed as the cost of various fees."

Yes, I agreed, Lincoln needed investment for handicapped accessibility and a new heating and air-conditioning unit. Huge cost of $13 million? More like $3 million was the estimate I obtained. A *Tribune* editorial noted my belief that cost estimates by Raymond had been "inflated beyond all reason" and observed that the administration "has neither made its case nor addressed the challenges to its plans." The possibility of building a new school at or near the present Lincoln site was also raised.

Raymond at the following board meeting was unhappy with both my observations and the editorial. She defended her cost estimates. The Lincoln principal who permitted the contractor to look at the roof for my estimate was transferred to another school. Coincidence in timing, no doubt.

But reason prevailed. Raymond and the board decided to rethink abandonment of the Lincoln site. They decided to build a new school at the Lincoln site to serve students at Lincoln and at another primary center, freeing space at the other center for vocational education. The old school was to be razed but not until the new one was ready. The neighborhood would not lose a school. That's what was important. My commitment was not to an old school but to the kids who attended. The new school has been built and is open.

A kind editorial in the newspaper commended me for standing up for Lincoln and praised Raymond, who now thank goodness has retired as superintendent, and the board for relenting and finally making a wise decision. I just provided a voice for some kids who had no input. Gayle Dantzler and the other editors at the newspaper provided another voice for the same objective. And the school board listened. They likely would not have heard the small voices of the little kids.

My intent certainly is not to try to run the schools, just to improve them. Real improvement cannot be accomplished by a superintendent, a board, or the teachers or the parents unless they work together, with the whole community involved. While improved facilities, expanded after-school programs, and more mentoring can help—really help, structural change in what is taught, particularly at the high school level, is essential to prepare our kids for the future.

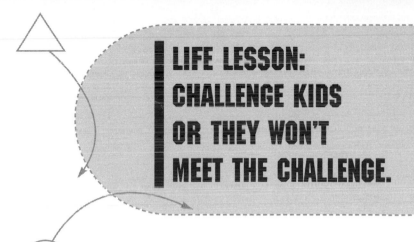

LIFE LESSON:
CHALLENGE KIDS
OR THEY WON'T
MEET THE CHALLENGE.

Chapter 27

High Schools: Warehousing, Not Educating

"Still, every freshman entering high school should be re-garded as a prospect for college and not be relegated to warehousing courses. Kids unchallenged can't be expected to meet a challenge never afforded. Kids who are challenged often rise to meet that challenge."

Twenty-seven

Our public schools have not adjusted to what's out there in the world today—the high-tech computer age and the challenge of the global economy. Teachers, try as they may, and most try very hard, cannot, as the schools are currently structured, prepare kids for either the present or the future.

In my own community of South Bend, a study showed that only 50 percent of the kids who begin high school go on to graduate. A 50 percent graduation rate! That is a disgrace. A disaster. And South Bend is not unique. Graduation rates are almost as bad or even worse in some of the other outdated high school systems around the nation.

Nationally, according to statistics cited by the National Governors Association for its 2005 conference on our troubled high schools, only 32 percent of kids who do graduate are ready to attend a four-year college. Where are the other 68 percent? For what are they ready? Many of our public school systems advance kids who are ill-prepared for high school. That's where mentoring and after-school programs can help. That's where community efforts such as the one we started at Lincoln School can make a difference.

Too many high school freshmen look forward not to a degree but to the age at which they legally can drop out. The value of education, more important than ever, is not instilled in the atmosphere at many high schools, where there is instead a situation of peer ridicule for taking study and education seriously. Courses don't provide a challenge, except for the unmet challenge to stay awake. Freshmen deemed in the system to be suited only for warehousing in "remedial" courses drift with others who lack enthusiasm for education. And darned if the evaluation of them doesn't come true. They don't make it.

Those who do make it to graduation often are not ready for college or for successful careers in the all-important trades and service-sector jobs where a college degree is not required. Everybody needs a high school degree. Everybody needs some post–high school education, whether in a trade, at a junior college, at a business or technical college, or in the military. Not everybody needs a college degree to be a success. A youngster who goes on to become the best plumber in town, an expert electrician, or an excellent carpenter, with or without a college degree, is successful, is filling a vital need, and can be well rewarded financially.

Still, every freshman entering high school should be regarded as a prospect for college and not be relegated to warehousing courses. Kids unchallenged can't be expected to meet a challenge never afforded. Kids who are challenged often rise to meet that challenge.

A high school student gets a message when placed in courses for low achievers and may well assume that striving for higher achievement, trying for college placement courses, would be silly. A kid labeled "stupid" is likely to act that way. Tell high school athletes or students involved in some other extracurricular activity that it requires only a passing "D" in courses to stay eligible, and they may well settle for a "D" awarded for just showing up in class. Tell them they lose eligibility for any grade lower than a "C," and you will find that most of them meet the tougher challenge and learn something—perhaps even learn to study and to develop a desire to do even better. Requirements for eligibility too often are now a joke and no favor to the high-schoolers who supposedly are given a break by the leniency.

Gangs in South Bend have been shooting it out, often with young men in their teens or early twenties wounded or dead. Teen violence at a once highly popular downtown summer festival brought demands to curtail it and finally resulted in its cancellation. A correlation between the terrible graduation rate and violence is obvious. Police note that most of the perpetrators are dropouts from high school. They can't get a job, ill prepared as they are for the workforce, but they can get a gun. Any kid can get a gun on the streets. They're everywhere.

They can join gangs. So they do, for recognition that has escaped them elsewhere and often for protection from other gangs. They can push drugs. And use drugs, sometimes committing crimes to afford an addiction.

Nor is it just the boys who get into trouble after dropping out of high school. Female dropouts have a much higher rate of unwed teen pregnancy than do the girls who stay in high school. They also are more likely to get involved with drugs. Crack babies can be a horrible result.

What happens to the smiling, cute little kids ages three, four, or five as they grow older, go through the school system, and become teenage terrors? Their environment? Their bad homes? Their bad neighborhoods? Okay. In a lot of cases, those factors are involved. But what are we doing about it? Preaching "family values" isn't the answer. Too many of these kids have no family of the type that I was fortunate enough to come from in Beacon. They may have no parents. Obviously, they had a father and mother in terms of their conception. They may, however, have neither father nor mother in their lives. They may be raised by a sibling, by an elderly grandmother, or by peers on the streets.

Are we finding mentors to work with some of these kids? Some. But not nearly enough. There are heartwarming stories emanating from mentoring programs, stories about lives turned around by adults taking an interest in kids from poor homes, poor neighborhoods, poor school systems, and giving them some guidance, some hope, somebody who actually cares about them.

In the decades of life, there comes a time for many of us after success has been achieved, whether we presently are retired or not, when we should give something back and try to make the world a little better place—perhaps just turn one life around for a child headed in the wrong direction or no direction at all.

Mentoring is rewarding. Associating with kids keeps you young. Many a sour old grouch would be rejuvenated by working with some kids and turning attention to the future of society rather than dwelling on woes and wrongs of the past. Think of the pride when a kid you helped invites you to high school graduation or college graduation. Think of the pride of involvement in a program to help an entire school.

The No Child Left Behind Act has a noble goal and had bipartisan support at its inception. Uniform testing standards in the act can provide more information on where our schools and our students rank. The testing shows, of course, that far too many children are being left behind. School systems complain that the act doesn't provide funds to help those left behind but actually penalizes schools with too many students who are behind.

One-size-fits-all testing doesn't take into account the vast differences in the student bodies of schools, the critics say. Now, also, political rhetoric and disputes cloud the future of the act. The situation is not hopeless, although it will be if communities don't address the problem, starting first with improving the public schools. The business sector, which has so much to lose if 50 percent of our kids are lost, needs to play a big part, participating in mentoring, investing in after-school programs, and demanding a change in the curriculum and school decorum to meet modern challenges.

While I have cited my Beacon upbringing as vital in whatever success I have obtained, my Beacon High School curriculum from then would be inadequate now. (I'm not even going to say a word here about Latin.) My tremendous advantage was having a mother and father who insisted on and instilled values. They never would have permitted me to drop out of high school. They and I always knew I would go on to college and get a degree. Sure, they thought that would lead to becoming a funeral director rather than directing a college basketball team. They and Beacon gave me the preparation I needed to pursue another goal.

As we stress science and math, we should not forget the importance in these times of global competition of knowing the globe. We laugh at the results of those quizzes in which high school students couldn't tell the Atlantic from the Pacific, couldn't identify the nations of Europe, and couldn't name the countries bordering us to the north and south. It's not a laughing matter.

If we are to maintain a democracy, students also need to learn the basics of government. How can you cast an informed vote if you don't understand that a state senator has nothing to do with confirming federal judges, that the mayor doesn't have a vote on saving or destroying Social Security, and your member of Congress doesn't have any jurisdiction over your trash pickup, snow removal, or state park operations? In other words, we still need basic education, including geography, history, and government.

Since I loved history—state as well as national and world—I'm amazed at how kids today relegate history to the "boring" category. The story of how we got to where we are today? Boring? Historic truth is more exciting than fiction. Is it the teaching? The texts? The lack of emphasis? We can't say it's all just the fault of the kids.

Bill Gates, the Microsoft chairman, talked about the deplorable dropout rates in a scathing evaluation of America's high schools at the 2005 National Education Summit on High Schools hosted by the National Governors Association in Washington. "America's high schools are obsolete," Gates told the governors and business executives at the summit. He said the high school systems "were designed fifty years ago to meet the needs of another age" and now are "limiting—even ruining—the lives of millions of Americans every year."

Gates was appalled that so many kids, particularly those from low-income families and minority groups, are channeled into courses that lack challenge, the ones I've referred to as warehousing courses, which provide no preparation for college and teach no skills needed to land a good-paying job. Gates rightfully branded this practice as "so offensive to our sense of equal opportunity that the only way the practice can survive is if we hide it."

We must confront it. Gates and other critics point out how we are falling behind other industrialized nations in education, particularly at the high school level, with lack of preparation in math, science, computer technology for global competition in this high-tech era.

Worse, there is virtually no preparation at all for the kids who will drop out and eventually inflate the crime rate, the unemployment rate, the prison costs, the unmarried teen-pregnancy numbers, and the welfare expenses. They will cost rather than contribute to society, and society had better do something about it.

Corporate America needs to wake up. What happens to productivity when a large percentage of the future workforce has no high school degree, just a little warehousing for a couple of high school years? The business sector must get involved—as Gates has done with his money and outspoken pleas—to provide assistance for promising, innovative programs, to encouraging executives and other employees to join in mentoring, and to demand a change in our high schools.

As Gates told the nation's governors, high schools designed a half century ago, before global competition and the high-tech era, simply are not what we must have today. It's as ridiculous a situation as it would be in basketball if some college coach today failed to recognize the addition of the shot clock and the three-point line. In education, we're not shooting the three-pointers in competition with other nations. We're letting the clock go off without even attempting a shot.

If a college had a coach who didn't instruct on how to use and defend against the three-point shot and who didn't bother to call attention to the shot clock, that coach would be replaced. When we have a high school system also out of sync with significant changes, we should replace it.

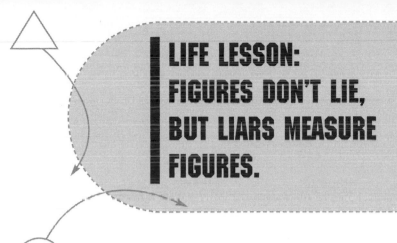

Chapter 28

The 2-Foot Yardstick

"In the job market, according to Census Bureau figures for 2004, the average wage for holders of a bachelor's degree was $51,206, and the figure for those with only a high school diploma was $27,915. Compare that with the average earnings of workers without even a high school degree, just $18,734. Education pays.

Education saves money, too. When graduation rates go up, crime-related costs go down. Graduates are less likely to commit serious crimes that cost society in money and pain and less likely to go to prison. It costs more than twice as much for incarceration of an inmate than it does for education of a student."

Twenty-eight

With so much concern about what our high schools are or aren't teaching and so much rhetoric about what education reform is or isn't accomplishing, there was keen interest in the Nation's Report Card on high schools issued in 2007 as part of National Assessment of Educational Progress evaluations. Passing grades? Well, there were disturbing test findings about measuring.

Here's the question: How long is a yardstick?

a. 3 feet

b. 2 feet

c. Not known for sure

d. All of the above

This is not one of those test questions on which a surprisingly large percentage of high school students give dumb answers. You know. Like picking the wrong countries to our north and south. This is a question about measuring the progress—or lack thereof—by the students. About the yardstick used. About its length. About whether there is test cheating, not by the students, but by the school officials through use of a 2-foot yardstick.

Yardstick length is in question as a result of two reports by the National Assessment people, who release what is commonly called the Nation's Report Card. Reports by these experts issued on February 22, 2007—based on the latest available data, for 2005 high school graduates—show an odd couple of findings.

The Nation's Report Card: America's High School Graduates showed seemingly great news. A review of transcripts of '05 high school graduates indicated that 68 percent completed at least a standard curriculum, up from 59 percent in 2000. Does this mean more kids are escaping the warehouse classes, the classes where they are stored until they can drop out? Does this mean more are getting a standard rather than substandard education?

This report also contained what seemed to be additional good news. The overall grade-point average for these graduates was about one-third of a letter grade higher than in 1990. The '05 graduates had an overall grade-point average of about 3.0, or about a "B." Back in 1990, it was only about 2.7. Does this mean we are making dramatic progress? Are kids learning more, doing better?

Now, the bad news from the other report. *The Nation's Report Card: 12th Grade Reading and Mathematics 2005* showed that these kids with fewer substandard courses and better grades also had the lowest average test scores on reading since 1992. The number at or above proficient in reading dropped to 35 percent, down from 40 percent in 1992. Less than a quarter of them scored at or above the proficient level in math. Also, data released earlier from *The Nation's Report Card: Science 2005* showed average scores in science testing decreasing since 1996.

What gives? How can students take tougher courses and get better grades but fail to improve in reading, math, and science? The use of a shorter yardstick appears to be the answer. Darvin M. Winick, chairman of the National Assessment Governing Board, which oversees the tests, said the findings "suggest that we need to know much more about the level of rigor associated with the courses that high school students are taking." In other words, do courses now labeled as "standard" measure up to what was defined that way in the past? Or have they been "dumbed down" so school officials can claim that more of their students are in a challenging curriculum instead of languishing in the warehouse? If so, warehousing by another name is not education reform.

"The reality is that the results don't square," Winick said.

Other members of the Assessment board also said that test scores should have gone up if more kids really were taking more rigorous courses. They also questioned how grades are being measured. Was that higher grade-point average due strictly to what is known as "grade inflation," giving higher grades through lowering standards for grades? If a 2-foot yardstick is used for measuring grades and the toughness of the curriculum, grades and curriculum will seem to be improved, but high school education won't really be any better.

In basketball, if we moved the three-point arc all the way in to the free-throw line, we'd have fantastic three-point shooting percentages and skyrocketing scores. But it wouldn't mean the shooting was any better. And we would have a lousy game.

We need more of a challenge in education and basketball, not just easier measurements. I've advocated moving our college three-point arc out to the more challenging distance in the international game. And I sure as heck want our high schools to make the courses more challenging, with standards at least as tough as in international competition in this global economy.

Some who don't want to admit we face a crisis in education sought to downplay the bad news of the reading test scores being the lowest since 1992. They pointed out that at least there was not much difference from 2002. Not much difference? That's the problem. We want a difference. As Winick said, "There is nothing good about a flat score." There isn't. Improvement should be expected. It's time to do more than talk about leaving no child behind as we continue to leave so many of them so far behind. It's time to do more than talk about narrowing the gap between white students and the minority students who so often are the ones warehoused, unchallenged, and left way behind.

The test showed a gap basically unchanged in reading skills since 2002. While 43.7 percent of white students were at or above the proficient level, only 20 percent of Hispanic students and 16 percent of black students reached that level. On the math test, 29 percent of white students achieved the proficient level, compared with only 8 percent of Hispanics and 6 percent of blacks.

We simply cannot compete with other nations in the global economy if we leave so many of our high school graduates so ill prepared. (And think also of the disgraceful percentage of kids who drop out, not even getting a high school diploma.)

John Engler, president of the National Association of Manufacturers, the nation's largest industrial trade association, summed up the danger succinctly in commenting on what he called the "disheartening" achievement scores. Said Engler: "We need young people who can adapt to the changing, high-tech workplace. In a modern facility, employees are more likely to be calibrating with a computer than pounding with a hammer. However, the skills needed to compete in a twenty-first-century workforce are just those that our graduates are having the hardest time achieving—math, reading, and science."

Engler said the test scores "echo the critical 'skills gap' manufacturers are facing" in trying to find quality employees. He warned that "our economy and way of life hinge on our ability to remain competitive."

What's needed? Engler, a former three-term governor of Michigan, said the tests are further evidence of the need to reform our high schools to "get the job done." To get the job done, corporate America is going to have to help. Engler, who pushed for education reform while governor, understands and articulates the problem. So does Bill Gates. But others in the business sector, from small businesses as well as from large corporations, need to join in a push for and an insistence on real reform, not just seeming reform as measured by a too-short yardstick. While nationally known corporate figures such as Gates can work for reform at the national level, getting the attention of Congress and the president, folks from small businesses—where qualified workers also are sorely needed—can work effectively for reform in their local communities. They can work with school boards, parents, teachers, and their state legislators.

More than speaking out is needed. Businesspeople should follow the lead of Gates in providing time and money. Not everybody, I know, can give even a smidgen of what Bill Gates can and does contribute to the cause of improving education. But you don't have to be rich to get involved with mentoring, with reading programs, with after-school activities, with supporting higher pay for teachers, with a fix-up, spruce-up project such as we had in South Bend at Lincoln School, or with letting school-board members and other officials know that you want real reform measured with a real yardstick.

To get the job done will require more than just concentration on making sure that high schools turn out higher-quality graduates. Quantity is vital, too. We must curb the terrible dropout rate. We need more as well as more highly qualified graduates. Among the many contributions to education by the Bill & Melinda Gates Foundation is a survey of why kids drop out of high school. Dropouts were asked why they quit school. Here are the five top reasons and the percentage citing each one:

— Classes were not interesting: 47 percent

— Missed too many days and could not catch up: 43 percent

— Spent time with people who were not interested in school: 42 percent

— Had too much freedom and not enough rules in my life: 38 percent

— Was failing in school: 35 percent

A key response, not surprising to me, was that 66 percent of the dropouts said they would have worked harder if expectations were higher. As I've maintained, kids who are challenged often rise to meet that challenge. Kids placed in the unchallenging atmosphere of warehousing classes sink to the level of that experience. They are the ones most likely to find classes not interesting, most likely to start missing too many days of school, most likely to spend time with other students who are not interested in school, most likely to drop out.

Too much freedom? Not enough rules? Again, I don't find it surprising that kids recognize the dangers of lax or lacking discipline. They want direction. They need rules, fair rules enforced with fairness. Rules should include a dress code. Uniforms have been found in some school systems to improve behavior at the elementary and junior high levels. If parents will go along, and they will if the purpose is properly explained, why not give uniforms a try?

For high schools and at the lower grades where no uniform is decided upon, there need to be stringent dress codes that prohibit exhibitionist, sloppy, or dirty attire. No clothing with gang symbols or references to drugs or alcohol. If kids can dress like whores or hoods, like druggies or cultists, like tramps or pimps, they may well act in character with their attire.

Random drug testing for students in athletics or in other extracurricular activities can be implemented, not to discourage participation but for the health and future of the participants. Again I stress the need to require those in extracurricular activities to keep up their grades. Tell high school athletes that any grade lower than a "C" will cost eligibility, and you will find that most meet the challenge. (Now, we also must get the schools to meet the challenge of having a "C" measured with a full-length yardstick.)

Let's also get physical education back into the role it deserves in our schools. Obesity in kids has increased, while the time allotted for physical education has decreased. Bullying cannot be tolerated. Athletes in particular must be watched by coaches, teachers, and school administrators for any tendency to bully. School shootings show the dangers of bullying, including fatal danger for those perceived as engaging in bullying. In the Columbine High School massacre in Colorado in 1999, the two teen killers, who apparently felt they were treated as social pariahs and ridiculed because of their trench-coat attire and unconventional attitudes, sought out the students with the white baseball caps traditionally worn by the athletes. One of the killers in his quest for targets even ordered at one point: "All jocks stand up!"

Now, I'm not suggesting that the athletes were responsible for the shooting. Of course not. Even if some of them did engage in ridicule of the trench-coat killers—and no doubt some did, probably thinking they were being funny, not being bullies— there is no justification for murder in retaliation. Still, guns are everywhere, and too many kids are armed and ready to respond to real or imagined disrespect by shooting. So schools need to be sensitive to potential conflict. The white caps may seem mostly to be good kids, and they probably are, but they cannot be allowed to push around fellow students who seem strange or troubled or even evil. Measuring tolerance for bullying should involve no differences over the yardstick length. Zero tolerance of bullying. For everybody's sake.

In addition to considering how student progress is measured, let's look also at a study measuring the college programs that turn out our teachers. *Educating School Teachers*, a report issued on September 18, 2006, by Arthur Levine, president of the Woodrow Wilson National Fellowship Foundation, says that the teacher education programs are inadequate. Levine, a former president of Teachers College, Columbia University, concluded that as many as three-quarters of the programs have inadequate curricula, low admission requirements, low graduation standards, faculty disconnected from K–12 schools, and insufficient quality control.

Among Levine's recommendations are these:

— Transform education schools into professional schools focused on classroom practice.

— Once the new teachers are in the classroom, make student achievement the primary measure of success of the programs.

— Rebuild programs around the skills and knowledge that promote classroom learning.

— Have five-year programs the norm, requiring every future teacher to complete a traditional arts-and-sciences bachelor's degree followed by a master's in a specific subject area.

— Close failing programs, expand quality programs, and create incentives to attract the best and brightest to teaching.

— Improve teacher salaries, with salary scales tied to teacher qualifications and performance to encourage the best teachers to stay in the classroom.

Not all the recommendations were greeted with enthusiasm by those involved in the operation and accreditation of the programs. But the report brought attention to the fact that no education reform is likely to produce quality results without quality teachers. Whenever there is a proposal to improve teacher salaries, there is debate over the question of whether a community can afford it. My question is whether a community can afford *not* to improve teacher salaries.

Getting and keeping the best teachers is vital in improving our schools and thus improving our workforce, improving our place in global competition, and improving our communities. We save money when we lower the dropout rate. With success in education—graduating from high school, going on to college, getting a degree—comes higher pay, less likelihood of being involved in crime, less need for welfare or other public assistance.

In the job market, according to Census Bureau figures for 2004, the average wage for holders of a bachelor's degree was $51,206, and the figure for those with only a high school diploma was $27,915. Compare that with the average earnings of workers without even a high school degree, just $18,734. Education pays.

Education saves money, too. When graduation rates go up, crime-related costs go down. Graduates are less likely to commit serious crimes that cost society in money and pain and less likely to go to prison. It costs more than twice as much for incarceration of an inmate than it does for education of a student.

For communities, good schools also are a key to economic development. Morton Marcus, director emeritus of the Indiana Business Research Center at Indiana University's Kelley School of Business, says that high schools "are the most important economic development tool in each community." In a lecture in Terre Haute, Indiana, Marcus said the best way for that city to promote economic development would be to have area high schools "rank among the very best in the state." As Marcus said, "Who wants to come to your community if your schools are known to be inadequate?"

Can't afford better education? You gotta be kidding. And we gotta stop kidding about measurements of progress in education reform.

That brings us back to that multiple-choice question at the start of the chapter on the length of a yardstick. The correct answer is (d) "all of the above." Well, that certainly seems to be the case when we evaluate the length of the yardstick used to measure how high school students are doing. The yardstick still is 3 feet long for the Nation's Report Card on those tests for reading, math, and science. Good. Sure seems that it's a 2-foot yardstick, at least in a lot of school systems, for measuring the strength of curriculum and grade-point average for graduates. Shame. And this means the length of a yardstick for all of this measuring is not known for sure. Intolerable.

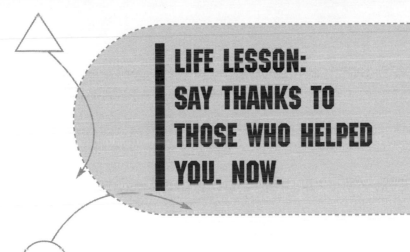

Chapter 29

Shut Up and Sit Down on the Bench

"What a shame it would have been if I had never told him what he meant to me, if I had never taken him to games where he could share in victories. Legendary Alabama football coach Bear Bryant once was to recite a simple line in a Bell South Telephone commercial to hype Mother's Day phone calls. "Don't forget to call your mama," he was to say. He ad-libbed a second line, "I wish I could call mine." There was a tremendous reaction to the coach's acknowledgment of his mother and his wish that she were still alive to receive a call from a grateful son."

Twenty-nine

While I've mentioned the decades of life in encouraging those in the later decades to consider mentoring and other efforts to help the kids, it is important also that those still in the earlier decades not forget people from the past who helped them and inspired them along the way. Family, of course. Also, for most of us there are others who came into our lives perhaps more briefly, such as a teacher who inspired, an employer who became a mentor, a member of the clergy who provided guidance at a time of past crisis, or a friend who was there when needed.

Sometimes those people drift away, never thanked for what they did, for what they meant. My thoughts were first of sadness and then of many happy times when I received word that Michael J. Scoba Sr. died on May 31, 2006, at age eighty-eight. He was one of the people who influenced my life back in Beacon. Mike Scoba was my high school basketball coach. His influence went beyond basketball. In fact, as I have noted, I never dreamed when I was a high school player that I would go into coaching. It wasn't a case of deciding, "Boy, I want someday to be a coach just like Mike."

But Scoba was someone I looked up to and respected from the time he came to Beacon when I was about nine years old. My first remembrances of Mike are of his teaching physical education at my grammar school and his coaching of youth baseball on the playgrounds during the summer. He also would teach and coach at Beacon High School. Mike, who played high school football in Colds Spring, a city south of us, was like a folk hero in Beacon. One reason was that he had been a football player at Syracuse University. Beacon was impressed to have a big-time Syracuse athlete come to coach. He was an assistant to another coaching hero, Jim Gauriloff, the head football coach. They led the Beacon High football team to an undefeated season in 1952.

Mike was a hero in ways beyond sports. He left Syracuse after his freshman season to enlist in the army. He participated in the Normandy landing and the rest of the campaign in Europe during World War II and was awarded the Bronze Star. He was always special to me, someone to look up to, a role model for how to strive for success and do things the right way.

On that undefeated football team coached by Gauriloff and Scoba, Corney Sadler was the quarterback—a black quarterback. What difference did his race make? None, to our coaches. That's the point. Back in 1952, even in the North, because of stereotyping, if not something more racist, it was rare for a black kid to play quarterback. Heck, much later, it was rare to see a black quarterback in college and professional football. Coaches at those higher levels still had the stupid misconception that a black quarterback wouldn't be accepted as a leader or would lack the smarts to run an offense. We didn't think anything of it. Sadler was the best quarterback. So he plays quarterback. Didn't have anything to do with skin color or religion or anything else.

Our coaches were indeed role models for doing things the right way. Their influence would have been with me, guiding me, whether I became a butcher, a baker, or an undertaker or, as happened, the coach at Notre Dame. Coaches can have a big impact on the lives of their players, just as teachers can influence their students. For kids who love sports, a coach sometimes has as much influence as parents—maybe even more these days—in keeping those youngsters in school and out of trouble.

Mike could be demanding, tough, as any good coach often must be. He also was appreciative of extra effort, such as when Caesar and I played defense with the intensity in basketball that pleased him and frustrated opponents. But he put up with no nonsense. I remember the time my junior year, on a day when we had no game, a bunch of us went to Wappingers Falls to see our rival play. They had a really good team that year. After seeing that game, I told Coach Scoba that I had a game plan to beat Wappingers Falls.

"Coach, I know how we can stop their best player," I excitedly proclaimed. "If we do this, we can beat those guys." I was jabbering on about what "this" was. Scoba looked at me. Looked at me. Just looked at me. And he wasn't looking with an expression of awe that his junior player knew what the coach should do. He then expressed the view rather firmly that I should stick to playing and leave the game plans to him. I don't recall the details of my game plan and have no idea if it was something that made sense and could have worked. At another time while I was on the bench during a game, I started offering coaching suggestions. Scoba responded as any coach would do: "Shut up and sit down on the bench." Even though I had no thought at the time of becoming a coach, I guess my instincts for analyzing strategy were with me even then.

While Mike had to make clear to the team that he, not some kid player, was in charge, he was free to be a friend and to talk basketball strategy with me after I graduated. Often when I came back home from college, I'd meet Mike at the Alps, the popular soda fountain where they had and still have the best chocolate in the world. I learned from Mike to love the game. Looking back, that love of basketball is what led me finally to the decision to continue to be a part of the game, to seek to coach, to seek to coach at Notre Dame.

My thoughts were indeed a mixture of sadness and memories of happy times when I heard that Mike had died. One of the happiest times ironically was at a Notre Dame defeat. Mike, I am proud to say, was a part of it. It came in a pivotal game early in 1971 as I was coaching Fordham to a 26–3 record and national prominence. I invited Mike and his wife, Barbara, to come to Madison Square Garden to see us play Notre Dame and the great Austin Carr. Caesar of course was there. In fact, a whole bunch of friends from Beacon came. But I wanted this to be special for Mike, a way to say "thank you" and let him know he had been important in my life and still was. The Garden was sold out. The place was up for grabs. We had taken New York City by storm. Tickets were going for big money. I was going for a big win. I also was going for the head-coaching job, my dream job, at the school we were playing, Notre Dame.

Now I was the coach. I could put in the game plan. And it was not a high school junior's plan to stop the best player on Wappingers Falls' team but a plan to stop Carr, the best college player in the nation. He had just scored forty-six points to nail UCLA with its last defeat before the start of that eighty-eight-game win streak. The few Notre Dame losses that season had come almost every time that an opponent used a zone defense.

We had not played a zone. For this game, we would. In doing so, we would surprise Notre Dame with a defense they did not think we would or could employ. We also would at every opportunity double-team Carr and dare other Notre Dame players to shoot from outside. When they took the dare, they often missed and deprived Carr of an opportunity to score. We won 94–88. Carr scored "only" twenty-nine, a lot, but well below his average and less than what Notre Dame needed.

Fordham won. So did I. With that win over Notre Dame, I won my dream job, coaching at Notre Dame. Nothing was certain that night, of course, but that victory was to be a key factor in Notre Dame's selection of me as coach for the following season. We celebrated, with Mike and Barbara Scoba traveling with Terry and me all the way as we visited parties all around New York City. Terry had driven them to the game.

At 2:00 a.m., we went to the Webster Bar, not far from the Fordham campus. It was a student bar, kind of like Corby's is in South Bend for Notre Dame students. When I walked in, the place went wild. I was pleased, of course. But I'd heard cheers before when we won big games. I was pleased most of all because Mike and Barbara, smiling, happy, and caught up in the enthusiasm, were there to share the moment with me. It was one way to say "thank you" and let Mike know that I wouldn't be there, hero of the moment, if it were not for his guidance and inspiration along the way.

He went to many other games, too. I didn't forget him. I never will. The last time I saw Mike in person was when I was back in Beacon, as I am every summer, for Caesar's golf tournament. I was riding with two of my best friends from Beacon, Mario and John Viniello. There he was, unmistakable, walking down Main Street and not looking anywhere near his age. "Stop, Mario," I hollered. "There's Mike Scoba." He was sharp as ever. He was then eighty-six.

What a shame it would have been if I had never told him what he meant to me, if I had never taken him to games where he could share in victories. Legendary Alabama football coach Bear Bryant once was to recite a simple line in a Bell South Telephone commercial to hype Mother's Day phone calls. "Don't forget to call your mama," he was to say. He ad-libbed a second line, "I wish I could call mine." There was a tremendous reaction to the coach's acknowledgment of his mother and his wish that she were still alive to receive a call from a grateful son.

Say thanks. Now. In a call, a letter, an e-mail, a personal visit, or some combination thereof. There were people who helped or inspired you along the way in earlier decades of your life. Don't wait until it's too late to call your mama. Don't wait until it's too late to thank a teacher, a coach, a long-lost friend. Thank God I was able to show my thanks to Mike Scoba and to bring him along to bask in the glory of that big basketball victory in Madison Square Garden. If I had not, news of his death would have brought just thoughts of sadness, not also the accompanying thoughts of happy times, such as when we celebrated in the Garden and all around the town.

**LIFE LESSON:
WE ALL GET
INVOLVED IN OUR
OWN WORLDS.**

Chapter 30

The "Real"
Dickie V

"There is, of course, a serious side to Dick. Times when he is serious about more than basketball. Times when he is quiet, concerned, contemplative. He is involved In all kinds of charity events and in providing scholarships. He and his wife, Lorraine, are proud parents of two daughters, Terri and Sherri, both of whom attended Notre Dame on tennis scholarships. Both graduated with MBA degrees. Dick provides annual scholarships at Notre Dame. He received an honorary degree from the university in 1997, and I've joked with him that if he just gave a little more, he could be the commencement speaker."

Thirty

"What's Dick Vitale really like?"

"How do you get along with Vitale?"

These two questions often are asked of me. Viewers see us together on ESPN, analyzing a big college basketball game or doing the show on NCAA Tournament pairings and assume that I have a perspective on the "real" Dick Vitale. They wonder if some of that "Dickie V" enthusiasm is faked, just an act. Also, they wonder if I find it exasperating at times to go on analyzing amidst a barrage of Vitale hype, hyperbole, and near hysterics over some team, some player, some shot, some matchup. Answers to those questions are simple, easy.

What's Dick like? What you see is what you get. He's the same guy off the air as he is before the camera. The intensity, the enthusiasm, the spirit are all real. It's not an act. It's what he is. He couldn't deviate from that persona if he wanted to. And he doesn't want to. He's genuine. Dick is really funny, without even realizing it at times. He just does and says funny things, before and after as well as during telecasts and even when he's just strolling around Notre Dame or having dinner with friends near campus at Parisi's Italian Ristorante.

How do I get along with Vitale?

"Awesome, baby!" We're teammates in television, not rivals. We're friends. Sure, he makes me laugh. He makes everybody laugh. Why not? College basketball is entertainment, a game, not World War III. But Dick doesn't just joke. He captures the drama, the excitement of the game. He highlights the highlights. And he knows the game. Dick was a highly successful coach before he went into television. His record as coach at the University of Detroit was seventy-eight wins and only thirty losses. With Detroit, he beat Al McGuire's Marquette team in the season when Marquette went on to win the national championship.

Nobody has done more for college basketball than Dick since he joined ESPN at the start-up of the sports network in 1979. Dick Vitale is the icon for college basketball. Television has played a major role in popularizing college basketball, in creating new fans. And the fans love him. When he arrives at a game site, fans start shouting, "Dickie V, Dickie V" and "Awesome, baby!" He provides energy for the fans and takes energy from their response. He will take time to talk with fans and to sign autographs, whether it's at courtside, at a parking lot, or at his table at Parisi's.

Funny without trying? Well, we'll be on a commercial break, ready on the set for the next segment, ready to go back on the air. Dick has a quick question for the producer and starts yelling, "I can't hear you. I can't hear you." The producer will say in my ear, "Digger, does Vitale have his earpiece in?" I'll look and say, "Dick, try your earpiece."

One year when we came in for NCAA championship week, in ESPN's Studio C getting ready for our broadcast, Dick is clearly distracted. He lost a button on his sports coat. He's frantic. "Dick, it's no big deal," I tell him. "We'll find you a button."

"But it's my button I want," he insists. "Gotta find my button."

He's on the phone, calling an airline, telling what flight he was on when he figures the precious button popped.

"Dick, the plane's left by now," I try to explain. "It's not like they're gonna bring the plane back with your button." He's just funny by accident, even when the accident is losing a button.

There is, of course, a serious side to Dick. Times when he is serious about more than basketball. Times when he is quiet, concerned, contemplative. He is involved in all kinds of charity events and in providing scholarships. He and his wife, Lorraine, are proud parents of two daughters, Terri and Sherri, both of whom attended Notre Dame on tennis scholarships. Both graduated with MBA degrees. Dick provides annual scholarships at Notre Dame. He received an honorary degree from the university in 1997, and I've joked with him that if he just gave a little more, he could be the commencement speaker.

When Dick's first grandchild was born in 2001, he wrote on ESPN.com that little Sydney Nicole Sforzo was presented immediately with a Notre Dame cap to designate her as "a Golden Domer from day one." He also wrote that I already had cleared the way for her to be in South Bend for her freshman year. Not quite. Not yet. But I bet she'll be a Domer.

One time when Dick and I were in New York for the "Jimmy V Basketball Classic," a fund-raising event to find a cure for cancer and named in honor of the late coach Jim Valvano, I spotted a familiar face in the crowd near Times Square. It was Bill Bennett, the well-known author and commentator who was secretary of education in the Reagan administration and drug czar for President George H. W. Bush.

"Bill," I called, getting his attention. I quickly introduced Dick and then began chatting with Bill, a man I knew from our association with President Bush and our mutual interest in education and drug policy. Dick is listening. As soon as Bill headed off in the other direction, Dick asked, "Who was that guy?"

"Dick, that was Bill Bennett," I explained, thinking maybe he hadn't caught the name and somehow hadn't recognized Bennett from TV. "He was secretary of education for Reagan. He was the drug czar for Bush."

"Oh, okay," Dick responded. Period. It was as though he had never heard of Bennett. Well, Dick's field is sports. This Bennett was from a different world.

Another chance meeting took place when I was a guest of former president Bush down in Texas in 2001. I was invited for a Friday speech by Lech Walesa, the Solidarity leader who became president of Poland, and for the Notre Dame vs. Texas A&M football game on the following day. On game day, that Saturday, I was riding with the former president as we pulled up in a motorcade at the site of a pregame lunch hosted by the A&M president. As we're getting out, I hear an unmistakable voice shouting, "Digger, Digger, Digger!" It was Vitale. He and Lorraine were there for the game.

"Come on over, Dick," I invited. I figured he wanted to get a photo with President Bush. He starts running over. I figured he was safe. No Secret Service agent was going to mistake the smiling, affable, well-known Dick Vitale as a threat.

"Bring Lorraine," I reminded him. Sometimes he needed such reminders.

I introduce them to the former president. They get a nice photo with their camera. Or at least they thought they did. It didn't turn out. Maybe Dick, in the manner of forgetting his earpiece, forgot to put in film.

As Bush and I headed into the lunch site, the former president turned to me and asked, "Now, who was that?"

"That's Dick Vitale," I explained. "He's famous on ESPN on college basketball. He's known for sayings like 'Awesome, baby!'" I couldn't help but think back to when Dick didn't know Bill Bennett. We all get involved in our own worlds.

Everybody calls him "Dick" or "Dickie V." Well, just about everybody. Lorraine calls him "Rich." Or if she is exasperated with him—you know, like if he's calling an airline for his button—she calls him "Richie." Sometimes, I'll call him "Richie." Just for fun. Almost any time with Vitale is fun. And funny.

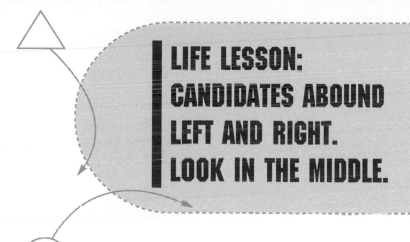

Chapter 31

Digger for President: What If He Ran?

"If I ran for president, it would be as a Democrat. I've always been a Democrat. Yes, I was a Reagan Democrat, and I was a Democrat who worked in a Republican administration. But I never left the party, even as I sometimes felt that some of the leaders of the party left me, moving in directions often far to the left, with which I couldn't agree. But neither could I move far to the right, where zealots claiming to be conservatives have pushed the Republican Party, alienating many segments of our population and abandoning the mainstream."

Thirty-one

If I ran for president, I'd be a long shot. A really long long shot. Kind of like the chances of ever becoming the head basketball coach at Notre Dame when I wrote that letter to Ara Parseghian back as a high school coach at St. Gabriel's in Hazleton, Pennsylvania.

Still, I've thought about running for president. Why? Well, when I look at some of the people who do run for presidential nominations, I have another question: Why not? Couldn't I do better than some of them? Don't some of them seem to put politics ahead of the people, their own welfare ahead of the general welfare, the wants of lobbyists ahead of the wants of the nation?

Also, the country needs a coach. Somebody who has a game plan to win the struggles we face now at home and abroad. Confronting the education crisis in this country is the biggest challenge in both domestic policy and in meeting global competition. We need a coach who can convince our people to work toward common goals, to mobilize in a "Domestic Storm" in the way that we once united in a "Desert Storm" to kick Saddam Hussein out of Kuwait. That kick, delivered with most of the world at that time with us, even led, as we know now, to Saddam's abandoning weapons of mass destruction. We were unified then. We need to be once again.

"We the People" should be our theme. "We the People," if unified, mobilized, and following a game plan to improve our schools, reward our teachers, and help our kids, could do wonders for the graduation rate, enhance the quality of learning, and curtail youth violence and drug use. A coach is needed, whether it be somebody with actual experience in coaching teams or a leader from another field who has a game plan and ability to organize and motivate. We need somebody as president to coach the nation.

I've thought about running for president. I even announced it once. Back in January 1995, during an interview with a reporter from the *Poughkeepsie Journal*, I said I was "going for it," for president, "angling for 2004." The interview came on the set of an ESPN studio in Bristol, Connecticut, during a break in my basketball analysis.

Ex-Notre Dame Coach Shooting for the White House was the headline for the resulting story. Another result was that the story was picked up by the news media nationally.

Not everybody rushed out to plaster "Digger in '04" bumper stickers on their cars when they read or heard the news. Actually, nobody did. Remember, this was back in 1995. Most of the comments in news stories about reaction to my "announcement" were filled with comments of surprise, skepticism, or jest. But the Poughkeepsie paper quoted one of the analysts who took it seriously and understood such an early expression of intent. George Mitrovich, president of the San Diego City Club and the Denver Forum, who was a press aide to Bobby Kennedy and wise in the ways of Washington, said this: "If you want to run for president, you have to make that determination a long time beforehand. There is a great need in this country to bring our diverse communities together, and I think Digger is uniquely qualified to do that."

I had in the past been mentioned as a possible U.S. Senate candidate in Indiana, and some people thought my decision to await the '04 presidential race was based on the desire first to win election to some other office as a stepping-stone for the White House. When I directed Operation Weed and Seed for the first President Bush, he told me that if I ever wanted to run for president I should first seek some other office. "You've got to be governor of Indiana first," he advised.

That was good advice in terms of building a political base and establishing credibility as an administrator. But I had no intention of running for governor, senator, U.S. representative, or any other stepping-stone office. Now, I'm not in any way belittling the importance of governors or members of Congress. However, serving in any office with desire to use it as a stepping-stone would for me be a matter of misplaced priorities and seeking a position for the wrong reasons. Run for governor because you have a burning desire to solve state problems, not to position for the White House. Run for Congress because of a burning desire to offer legislative solutions, not out of ambition to build a political base for higher office.

Good people can use and have used stepping-stone offices along the way in contending for president. It should also be possible to run for president with other qualifications outside the world of politics, qualifications that include a burning desire and game plan for helping America to solve some of its most pressing problems. Presidents have in the past come to serve without a base of holding an elective office. Is it still possible to do so? Maybe.

Unfortunately, one thing that is not possible is to be a serious contender for president without huge amounts of campaign funding. Up-front money is needed to hire the campaign staff and the fund-raisers who amass even more money for all the costly TV purchases necessary to compete in all the presidential primaries that now are jammed together early in the nomination process.

If a candidate for president doesn't have millions ready for the start of the primaries, the news media and the political powers will brush off that candidate as having no chance. And the brushing off means there is no chance.

As the time came to decide on whether to actually run in '04, I decided against it. The thought of trying to raise the millions upon millions of dollars needed to run, with countless hours just "dialing for dollars," calling the big donors to plead for contributions, wasn't appealing. Also, President George W. Bush, son of my friend and former White House employer, was seeking a second term and highly popular in the early polls as a result of the initial military success in Iraq. I had no intense incentive to run against him.

If I ran for president, it would be as a Democrat. I've always been a Democrat. Yes, I was a Reagan Democrat, and I was a Democrat who worked in a Republican administration. But I never left the party, even as I sometimes felt that some of the leaders of the party left me, moving in directions often far to the left, with which I couldn't agree. But neither could I move far to the right, where zealots claiming to be conservatives have pushed the Republican Party, alienating many segments of our population and abandoning the mainstream.

If I ran, I would indeed run as a Democrat, not a left-wing, liberal Democrat, of course, but as a Reagan Democrat who would hope to win with support of moderates in both parties, including Digger Republicans. I would, for example, support a constitutional amendment to ban desecration of the American flag. I proudly fly the flag at my home. And I disagree with Democrats who have opposed the amendment to protect the Stars and Stripes.

I've thought about '08.

If I ran for president, I'd urge a national commitment to education, starting with preschool programs to get the kids, especially those from disadvantaged environments, off to a better start. I'd call for a strong foundation in math, English, and reading skills in early grades. I'd denounce the relegating of too many high school students to warehousing and the deplorable dropout rate. I'd pledge to use the bully pulpit of the presidency and tax incentives to encourage the business community to work with public education for the mentoring and after-school programs I deem so vital in saving kids who otherwise will be lost as productive citizens.

School buildings should be open from 8 a.m. until 5 p.m., including time for after-school programs, the programs needed to keep kids off the streets in those danger times right after dismissal. Teachers should be paid better, especially with longer hours for those directing the after-school programs. Solution?

Why not get average teaching salaries up to $48,000, with corporate America through tax write-offs contributing toward $10,000 of the additional after-school-program pay?

We must find ways to afford education improvements because we can't afford as a nation not to do so. Better education provides huge long-term benefits. A Center for American Progress task force report on education, "Getting Smarter, Becoming Fairer: A Progressive Education Agenda for a Stronger Nation," found there would be remarkable returns on education investments. They estimated that a 1 percent increase in high school graduation rates would produce savings of approximately $1.4 billion annually in the cost of crime, or about $2,100 for each male high school graduate. They also estimated that early intervention programs save society from $30,000 to $100,000 per child.

If I ran for president, I'd talk about all of that. About the cost of doing something and about the much higher cost of doing nothing. Why doesn't every presidential candidate talk about these pressing education problems and offer the solutions that can be implemented?

We need more discipline in schools, dress codes, random drug testing where necessary, requirements for community service by middle and high school students, and more, not less, time for physical education and physical activity at recess to alleviate childhood-obesity concerns. Yes, I know a president can't order local school boards to institute dress codes and some of these other things. And shouldn't. Nor would I advocate that Congress pass legislation to usurp local decision making in details of curriculum and conduct. But a coach—a president—can rally national support, can demand, and can bring about constructive change.

Again, a president couldn't and shouldn't set local policies for grade averages needed for eligibility to participate in extracurricular activities, including sports. But what about the impact of a president in the State of the Union Address telling the nation that the time has come to require that middle and high school students who want to play sports, be cheerleaders, play in the marching band, or work on the school newspaper must have no grade lower than "C" if they want to continue with those extracurricular pursuits? Let me say it again, stress it again: Tell kids that they are still eligible with a "D" average or even with an "F" in some course, and they have little incentive to do better. Give them a challenge to do better, and if the extracurricular activity means anything to them, they will meet the challenge.

If I ran for president, I'd talk about Mexico, not as a problem but as a trading partner whose potential has not been realized. Wal-Mart imports a large percentage of its merchandise from China. Why can't we instead make Mexico our China? The North American Free Trade Agreement (NAFTA) is supposed to be a partnership for trade between Canada, the United States, and Mexico. It should be just that, with Mexico encouraged to reach its economic potential and provide more merchandise and, in the process, to create more jobs for its people. More jobs there would help to alleviate the illegal immigration concerns in this country. I'm talking about jobs with decent pay. Decent pay helps the economy. Henry Ford started paying his workers $5 a day in 1914, a large amount at the time. One of his goals was to enable those employees to be able to afford to buy the cars that they made. It worked.

If I ran for president, I'd talk about bringing health-care costs down. How? By calling a summit meeting bringing together representatives of pharmaceutical firms, the medical and legal professions, hospitals, insurance companies, and consumer groups. None of these want poor health care. But often in protecting their own interests they hinder implementation of ways to improve care and lower costs. Let's get them together, with the nation focused on their efforts, to find solutions that could be acceptable to all sides.

If I ran for president, every political analyst would say I would lose. Sure, I know what a long, long shot I would be. But you can't lose in running for president, except in vote counts, if you have an opportunity to present views that could become part of the national dialogue and eventually become national policy, no matter who winds up in the White House.

Chapter 32

Four Good Friends, Soon to Be Three

"Among the toughest tasks of my life has been delivering eulogies four times at funerals—for my father, for my mother, for Caesar, and for Bill Hickey, a friend who was a director of food services at Notre Dame and much, much more."

Thirty-two

What a beautiful weekend in Beacon, that first weekend in August of 1994, with the weather cooperating to enable my buddy Caesar; two of our closest friends, twin brothers John and Mario Viniello; and me to play golf, a lot of golf, as we always did when I came for a summer visit. It wasn't just golf. It was camaraderie. Four friends getting together to catch up on what was happening. Four friends to reminisce about good times, great times, and troubled times. Four friends to joke, to challenge, and to ridicule missing a putt or hitting a tree. Four good friends soon to be three.

Tradition called for Caesar, Johnny, and Mario to meet me at Stewart Airport in Newburgh. They'd bring a six-pack. On the route to Beacon, we'd catch up quickly on any big events in our lives, and then, if time permitted, we'd get in a few whacks at that little white ball.

For this weekend, I arrived on a Thursday, early enough for us to head to the course at Southern Duchess Country Club. Johnny couldn't make it on that Thursday. Just Caesar, Mario, and me.

Anybody who plays golf, and probably those who don't, will understand my frustration after I hit three brand-new balls into water hazards. "Gosh," I was saying. "Heck, anyway." Or something like that. You know. Words I'd use as a coach when players didn't hustle. I'm really upset. Mario starts laughing. Mario's really laughing. Why not? We always zinged each other in one of those great relationships where we could and would joke about our faults and urge each other on to our strengths. I was really angry over losing my balls, golf and beyond, in this macho mix of friends.

"Come on, Mario," Caesar said. "It's only Thursday. Let's not get Digger started yet. Or it's going to be war over a long, long weekend."

That night we ate at an Italian restaurant in Beacon that's a favorite. I ate too much. We all did. Next morning, Caesar picked me up for our Friday golf rounds. That last spicy meatball, he thought, might have led to indigestion that woke him up at 3:00 in the morning. On the way to the course, Caesar stopped at a gas station. He came back with a bag of apples. "Hey, Caesar, apples for a snack?" His usual snack was a cheeseburger with bacon and mayonnaise.

We played on Friday. We played on Saturday, a beautiful day. We played eighteen holes. Came in for lunch. Went back for another eighteen. Then Caesar and I headed for the nineteenth hole—the bar at the clubhouse—to relax, to cool off with a cool one.

Caesar emerged from the restroom to tell me abruptly, "I don't feel good. Let's go." Maybe he caught a bug. Maybe that indigestion the other night was a sign of this virus or whatever it was coming on. Maybe that's why he decided to eat apples. We walked to the parking lot for the car so that I could take Caesar home. Then he said in a way that really frightened me, "I really don't feel good." Maybe it was something worse than a bug.

"Sit down right here," I told Caesar. "I'll get help." I rushed back to the clubhouse, where a call was made for an ambulance after a quick decision not to risk taking him to the hospital in a car. I called Helene, his wife. She got to the course with a daughter and son-in-law as the ambulance arrived. Caesar characteristically decided to walk to the stretcher, not await its arrival to him. Helene got in the front of the ambulance to go with Caesar.

Suddenly she was out of the ambulance, panicked, coming up to me to say the paramedics had started working frantically on Caesar in the back of the ambulance. "Digger, there's something seriously wrong," she said. "The way they're working on him. They're beating on his chest."

The ambulance raced off to the hospital in Newburgh. Driving there by car seemed to take a week. I feared that Caesar had died. At the hospital, we found that the frantic efforts had failed. Caesar had suffered a massive, fatal heart attack. That beautiful day became one of the roughest of my life.

It was like losing a brother. Caesar had been a part of my life since we were kids at South Avenue Grammar School. There was a hilly street near his home, and we would go sledding there in the winter. And then it was together in sports on teams in high school. He was a much better football player. I gave up football in high school when it became clear that I tripped over my own knees in the backfield. We both played basketball for Coach Mike Scoba, both of us perhaps lacking a bit of finesse but with a determined, physical style. There was a picture in the yearbook of Caesar and me sandwiching an opponent on the court. We could do that very well.

And, of course, I gave him the nickname of Caesar in high school in honor of his inability, similar to mine, to pass the Regents Latin test in repeated efforts. So Normington Schofield Jr. had become Caesar to us, to his friends, although others called him Norm and his parents called him Normie.

I always kept in touch, inviting Caesar to attend when he could our games at Fordham and then our Notre Dame games in the East. He was there with me to celebrate at Fordham when we beat Notre Dame. As I noted earlier, he did miss our breaking of the UCLA win streak but still was thrilled that day, telling me on the phone, "That's nothing. We beat St. Joachim's!" Coaching a kids' basketball team in Beacon was as important to him that day as coaching anywhere at any level.

We went into coaching at the same time, he as an assistant in football. He did not coach beyond the high school level, although I tried for a time to convince him to move to college coaching. "Caesar, you can do college football," I'd tell him. "You should give it a try. Apply to be an assistant someplace." I would have used any contact anywhere to help Caesar find that place.

He never wanted to move on or up in coaching. He was happy teaching and coaching where he was, happy with family life with Helene and his kids and with all the people he knew and helped in so many ways. And that was great. When I talk of setting and seeking goals, I never want to suggest that everyone must shoot for the moon and then feel dejected because it wasn't within reach. What's important is to have some constructive goal and work toward it, whether it's to be a good physical-education teacher, which Caesar was, or to be a college Latin professor, something to which neither he nor I could or would ever aspire.

Not only did Caesar do what he enjoyed, he added to the enjoyment for himself and for those around him by doing it well. Like coaching those kids from St. John's to the school's first win in years over St. Joachim's in a Catholic Youth Organization league.

While I learned early in life as an undertaker's son about the reality of death and about what must be done by the living when death strikes a loved one, none of this lessened how shocking and rough it was on that day when Caesar died. We started calling people with the bad news—his kids, my kids. I called Terry and my sister Diane, who had gone to Kennebunkport to have lunch that day with Barbara and George Bush. Other calls to those who needed to know. You try to break the news gently, but how can you, really, when the news, no matter how worded, will be heartbreaking, the way your own heart is breaking.

Helene asked me to give the eulogy. Of course I would. For Caesar. For Helene. But how could I put into words what Caesar meant to so many, including me, and do it in a way Caesar would want and without total loss of composure?

"Caesar lived life for people," I said. "He touched us all in his own special way."

Indeed he did, as shown by the line extending around the block at the funeral home on the night of his wake. I stressed his kindness. He was the kindest guy. Looking back, perhaps that indigestion Caesar suffered could have been a warning sign, perhaps a slight heart attack. Perhaps his uncharacteristic purchase of apples for a snack was an indication that he realized he should improve his diet. But as a physical-education teacher, a former athlete, and a coach, he no doubt believed exercise on the golf course would be beneficial.

Perhaps it was inevitable, a genetic determination that decreed that Caesar would die at age fifty-two. His family had a history of heart ailments. His younger brother, Little Caesar, had died of a heart attack, ironically, on a golf course as well. An uncle died of a heart attack. There were others in a hereditary pattern. Perhaps that was one of the reasons he was so active with the American Heart Association, chairman of the local effort. He also was instrumental in bringing the "Jump Rope for Heart" program to the school system where he taught.

Perhaps, if you believe God sets a specific time, He rewarded Caesar for his kindness by letting him first enjoy a beautiful weekend, doing what he loved, golfing together. One more time for four good friends.

Three good friends—John and Mario Viniello and I—now golf every summer in the annual memorial golf event in honor of Caesar. Every year, since Caesar's death in 1994, it has financed college scholarships for deserving students from three area high schools.

Among the toughest tasks of my life has been delivering eulogies four times at funerals—for my father, for my mother, for Caesar, and for Bill Hickey, a friend who was a director of food services at Notre Dame and much, much more.

While I have no copy of the eulogy for my father, I hope this undertaker's son has presented clearly my love and admiration for him in this book. I also have sought to show similar feelings for my mother and for Caesar. I do have excerpts from remarks in Caesar's eulogy and the full eulogy for my mother and for Bill, a friend I hope to introduce now to readers through the printing of my eulogy at his funeral.

Excerpts from the eulogy for Normington Schofield Jr.: Caesar

Caesar lived life for people. He touched us all in his own special way.

It's sad that others coming along now won't be touched by him. Yet, we can learn from what he did and do it the way he did.

If each one of us would care about others, as Caesar did, and reach out as he did by action and words of kindness, love and understanding, neighborhood by neighborhood, there would be peace in the world.

President Kennedy stated some thirty years ago, while Caesar was in college: "Ask not what your country can do for you, but what you can do for your country."

Caesar lived that for people.

The eulogy for my mother was written in my kitchen, with many tears, as I awaited the flight the next day that would take me on a sad journey home. My father had died twelve years before. My tears flowed then as well. Now, there was an additional feeling to go along with the sadness, a feeling of loneliness, a feeling that now I, as my father had been, was an orphan. I had no living parent.

This may not be an unfamiliar feeling after the death of the final living parent. A friend of mine expressed that same sentiment after the loss of both parents. "I feel like an orphan," she said. After my mother died, so did I.

Eulogy for Maggie, my mother, on December 12, 2004

If a name could say it all then Maggie is the name. Born Margaret Adele Sullivan on April 18, 1918. Her life touched many in many ways.

Her mother's parents, immigrants from Ireland named Timoney, helped build New York City in the late 1800s and into the early 1900s by making 250,000 bricks a day at Timoneyville Brick Yards, a few miles south of Beacon on the Hudson River. Eventually the business failed during the Depression.

Maggie's father ran an Irish bar in Bank Square a few blocks from here, but never drank. She was the youngest with two older brothers, Francis and James Sullivan. Francis, a great basketball player in the '20s, not only in Beacon but in the Hudson Valley, died of a blood blister from playing basketball because penicillin was not around at the time. She never had a Christmas after Francis died around the holidays, until she met Dad in the late '30s. The Irish mourned that way back then.

James worked at Rosa's furniture store on Main Street, but was a politician as county supervisor until he died in 1969.

When Maggie graduated from Beacon High School in the mid-'30s, she went to nursing school at St. John's University. But that fall, her mother wanted her back in Beacon to help at her home—13 Cottage Place—to run a rooming house.

In 1938, Richard Bruce Phelps came to Beacon to work for Fred Hignell as an assistant funeral director at 10 Willow Street. He lived in a rooming house in the backyard of the funeral home, next to 13 Cottage Place.

Yes, Margaret and Dick Phelps married and had three children, Richard, Diane, and Barbara.

When Fred Hignell died, Dad bought the 10 Willow Street funeral home. Maggie and he became a team.

Dad was a perfectionist, a stern and caring person for the city of Beacon. A community leader, he did a lot of projects, helped build a Little League field, a swimming pool for the country club, ran an Aunt Jemima pancake breakfast for Kiwanis, as well as serving on a community urban renewal board.

Maggie was Beacon's First Lady. She was known for her cute wit, sense of humor and being a prankster—although she would always deny the act. She had a charisma that everyone in the community loved. Maggie never finished nursing school, but she was destined to be a nurse in a different way. For three days she would nurse a family that had lost a loved one, as they grieved in their pain, until the funeral's end. She would spend hours at the wake in the funeral home giving the family tenderness and compassion to get them through this difficult time.

She also volunteered at Highland Hospital, would say hello to everyone on Main Street and was a volunteer parent for the CYO when we were teenagers, especially at dances to make sure I was behaving.

Our parents taught us that life was precious, people were equal and that all cultures, religions, and color of skin were one. And that people trusted us, the Phelps family, to help them through the loss of a loved one.

They mentored us on how to live and give back in the game of life. We were lucky to have them as parents. Diane, a teacher, and Barbara, a nurse—we chose our journeys in life with Mom and Dad as our role models.

As a grandmother to Karen, Rick, and Jen, little did she know that her influence would carry on to them and to all her great-grandchildren. Maggie's last six years were especially blessed by Diane and her husband, Kirk, being close by, caring for her when she moved to the Boston area.

This last Christmas in Seattle, we knew Maggie was in a bad place. I was holding McCabe on the couch at Karen and Jamie's. I said to Karen, as I laid McCabe on his back, watching him kick his feet, wave his arms and hands and making noises: "McCabe is five months old, just coming into his world, as Maggie, at eighty-five, is fading out." Life's journey is so strange.

Dad died twelve years ago. As Maggie leaves her journey here on Earth, they finally will be together again as Maggie comes home to join him in their eternal life together.

William J. Hickey Jr., my friend Bill, director of food services at Notre Dame, died after jogging in Colorado Springs on the weekend of the Notre Dame football game with Air Force in

1989. With all he did so well for our events and the needs of the team, he was like an assistant coach for Notre Dame basketball.

Jim Gibbons, a Notre Dame administrator, and I arranged for Bill's casket to be brought back to South Bend on the plane carrying the football team home. Notre Dame was home for Bill as well. He loved the university, and it showed in all that he did.

Eulogy for William J. Hickey Jr., my friend Bill, on October 17, 1989

There have been many legends of Notre Dame—Rockne, Gipp, Leahy, Ziggy. In the administration with Bill Burke. In the faculty with Frank O'Malley, Joe Duffy. In the CSC order with Frank and John Cavanaugh. Jim Schilts. Tom Brennan. Mike McCafferty. Bill Toohey, who died on October 13, 1980.

Legends leave their trademark, their expertise. Bill Hickey was no different than those I've mentioned and many others I didn't mention. He was committed to Notre Dame.

Think about it. Bill was born back East right after the Rockne era and grew as a young boy during the Leahy era. Probably listened to Bill Stern on radio doing the Army–Notre Dame games or snuck into Yankee Stadium or the Polo Grounds to watch Notre Dame play. Like many Catholics with Irish blood, Bill dreamed of either going here as a student or working here as an adult. Once he got here some eight years ago, the dream became reality.

His creativity with functions was like Vincent Van Gogh masterpieces. He did things the only way he knew how. First Class. High Quality. And the best service. When he would run a function, it would be like an invasion. The trucks would come rolling in with equipment, supplies, and as many troops as needed to set up the event. From start to finish, there would be General Hickey covering all flanks or in battle himself to make sure it was done right: The Hickey way.

After the event you would see him, white shirt and tie, driving the forklift reloading the trucks. It would be nothing for him to do eight events during a weekend and still make sure the dining halls were feeding over 20,000 meals daily to the students, faculty, and staff. He built his own coliseum or stadium—the North Dining Hall—upper deck, lower deck, sky box, it's all there. He felt he wasn't appreciated at times, yet those who really knew him would tell him he was wrong. He was such a perfectionist he would overdrive himself. It will take the energy of five people to replace him.

Can you visualize him last Friday at the Gates of Heaven in his jogging outfit, running by St. Peter, yelling: "Hickey, William J. Jr., Notre Dame!" Heading right to the poker table with the other Notre Dame legends, saying: "Move over fellas and deal me in." Rock asking, "Didn't you bring anything to eat?" Hickey with his walkie-talkie: "Food Service One to base. Send up some pizzas."

He dreamed it. He lived it. He died Notre Dame!
William J. Hickey Jr.

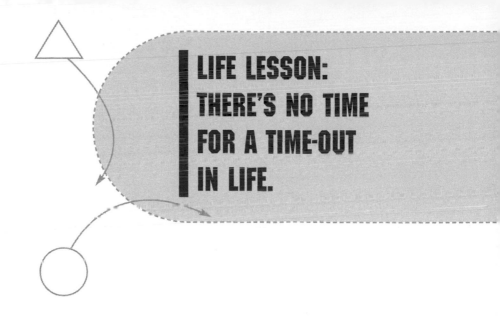

**LIFE LESSON:
THERE'S NO TIME
FOR A TIME-OUT
IN LIFE.**

Chapter 33

No Decade to Waste: Do It Yesterday

"Back at the funeral home in Beacon, growing up in the 1940s and '50s and into the '60s, I noticed how often some hardworking man that we knew, maybe some guy who toiled in a factory and even at a second job to get kids through college, finally would retire at age sixty-five and move to Florida. He would come back to our funeral home in a box a year or two later.

'That's wrong,' I thought. 'Retiring shouldn't be like the first stage of death.'"

Thirty-three

As an undertaker's son, seeing how life's journey oft comes to an unexpected end, with goals unfulfilled, I developed a philosophy of life for the decades of living. First, always live life to the fullest. I repeat my earlier admonition: Do it yesterday. Tomorrow might not come.

Now, I don't mean that life should be led recklessly or without goals for tomorrow. Far from it. Young people need to set goals, to dream. My goal, my dream, as I told Ara Parseghian in that letter in 1965, when I was coaching at St. Gabriel's High School, was to be the head basketball coach at Notre Dame. At age twenty-nine, I reached that goal.

Good fortune and the right contacts were involved but so was determination to be ready, to take shortcuts to get to the top, to avoid years as a high school coach, year after year as an assistant college coach, and then more years as head coach at a small college. My shortcut was to attend the camps and study the techniques of the masters of college coaching, the veterans who knew how to do it. Learn fast to move fast.

Would I have been bitter, angry, or despondent if I had not reached that ultimate goal? Would I have written my life off as a failure? Of course not. There are myriad worthwhile, satisfying endeavors.

When my sister Diane was asked by a reporter what she thought I would have done if I had not gone into coaching, she said, "Oh, he probably would have been governor of New York." Diane is quite kind in estimating her brother's ability. I've never thought about what I would have done if I had stayed in New York and not gone into coaching. I do have an intense interest in government. Perhaps I would have pursued a political career. Whatever I might have done, it would have been in an all-out effort to reach a worthwhile goal.

Have a dream and pursue it, I advise young people. Shoot for your ultimate goal. If you don't, you have no chance of attaining it. If you do, you just might get there or at least ascend way up the ladder toward it. Goals don't have to involve a quest for fame or fortune. Not everybody would welcome fame or be interested in seeking a fortune. Becoming a damn good electrician, carpenter, or plumber can be a worthwhile goal, bringing a good lifestyle, decent compensation, and the satisfaction of providing skilled, vital services.

After the first two decades of life, the formative years, the time from ages twenty to thirty is when to find the right career and lifestyle to suit our needs and to set and shoot for our goals. While my goal was reached at Notre Dame at age twenty-nine, it can, of course, take longer as life continues over the next twenty years, a time to go get it done. For many, those also are the years to raise and educate children and look ahead, not to just sitting around in retirement but to continuing life in what can be interesting, rewarding new directions.

My philosophy, rooted in observations of life and death in Beacon and more fully developed now as I grow older, encompasses what I consider three of the most important decades in life—ages fifty to sixty, sixty to seventy, and seventy to eighty. Not everybody will be fortunate enough to live all those decades and do so in good health, but anyone who does should not waste those years.

Back at the funeral home in Beacon, growing up in the 1940s and '50s and into the '60s, I noticed how often some hardworking man that we knew, maybe some guy who toiled in a factory and even at a second job to get kids through college, finally would retire at age sixty-five and move to Florida. He would come back to our funeral home in a box a year or two later.

"That's wrong," I thought. "Retiring shouldn't be like the first stage of death. There has got to be a way that this doesn't happen to me." The impact has never left me. Even if new administrators at Notre Dame had not decided they wanted a new basketball coach of their own, forcing my departure, I would not have remained in coaching much longer. I had determined that soon after age fifty, I would leave coaching to pursue and develop other interests. I saw the decade from fifty to sixty as a time to enrich life, not start a drift toward an inactive retirement that would be an invitation to end up too soon in one of those boxes.

During that decade of my life, I was able to work as a presidential appointee in a war on drugs, gangs, and violence; to go to Cambodia as a U.N. election observer; to represent the president in an official visit to Ghana; and still to be involved with basketball as a TV analyst. I can control my life, with basketball still important, without basketball controlling me. With ESPN, I basically work five months during the basketball season and then have seven months off to do what I would like.

What I have liked includes painting and pursuing my fascination with the great artists, especially Van Gogh, as I visit museums and art institutes here and abroad. What I have liked includes gaining more appreciation for music, including symphonies. If I had still been coaching and recruiting seven days a week or working year-round on television, I would not have had time to attend and develop fondness for symphonies and listen more to all types of music with which to dream, visualize, fantasize, think things through, get motivated, or just relax. What I have liked includes attending Broadway productions and playing a lead part in the play *Love Letters*, not on Broadway, but in summer theater in Maine and at Notre Dame's historic Washington Hall.

What I have liked includes time spent with children and grandchildren, with frequent trips to Seattle to see the Moyers—my daughter Karen and son-in-law Jamie Moyer, he of major league pitching fame, and their six children—and hearing proudly of their philanthropy. The Moyer Foundation has raised over $8.5 million to support more than one hundred different organizations that help children in distress. What I have liked includes promoting mentoring and after-school programs to help kids stay in school and stay out of trouble. What I have liked includes seeking better schools. That means more community involvement to press for better education than the warehousing in high schools. It also means projects such as our effort to help the kids in the Lincoln School area in South Bend.

What I have liked includes annually singing "Take Me Out to the Ballgame" during the seventh-inning stretch at a Chicago Cubs game. What I have liked includes time to visit the Farmer's Market in South Bend, a place to chat with shoppers and proprietors and find great produce at reasonable prices, and time just to hang out at Parisi's Ristorante and talk with folks from Notre Dame—athletes, coaches, priests, and professors, as well as visiting sports figures and fans and people from all walks of life.

I could do more television, make more money. I could have gone back into coaching. No thanks. Now, as I'm into that next decade, sixty to seventy, my goal is to travel, not to Florida to retire, to die. But to places I haven't seen around the world. I've been many times to England, France, and Yugoslavia and would like to return. More recently I traveled for the first time to Australia to attend the seventieth-birthday bash for Basil Sellers, a friend who rose from nothing to become a multimillionaire and philanthropist. In a way it was kind of a living wake. Basil heard his friends say all those nice things about him while he still was alive to hear the accolades.

There also are charity golf tournaments, always the one for Caesar. But not everybody, I'm well aware, can afford to travel abroad while living on a fixed pension, Social Security, and perhaps a little outside income—maybe even without any pension these days. Travel in this country can be as rewarding, however, particularly if it includes visiting with children and grandchildren and old friends.

Important in all this is to stay in physical shape. That's why when I'm in South Bend I go to Notre Dame to work out three or four days a week—fifty minutes on a Stairmaster, occasionally showing up some young college athletes who can't keep up the pace. You can't just sit all day on a couch watching junk on television and expect to remain in shape to do some of the other things that are more interesting, more stimulating, more worthwhile. Associating with young people is important for me. You think young, act young, and you are young, or at least younger in your attitude and approach to life.

While I stress travel goals for ages sixty to seventy, that doesn't mean someone has to sit home in the decade of ages seventy to eighty. Slow down? Sure, if need be. Still, don't retire. Don't retire from life. This decade is one where it is possible to take years of wisdom and experience and put them to use in a positive way. Mentors can change the lives of youngsters who otherwise will head in the wrong direction or drift in no direction at all.

Productive, interesting life in that decade of seventy to eighty is like icing on the cake. If I am fortunate enough to reach that age, I'd like to do something like go to Tuscany, rent a villa, live at a vineyard for a week, see how it's done. Jamie once said that when he's done with baseball, he'd like to do that, too. Maybe we can.

Anything over age eighty is a bonus. You can't count on it, but make the most of it if you are granted so many years. I admire people I know at Notre Dame who still, in their eighties, take trips and lead students on trips abroad. Just don't ever retire. Restart. Find things that give you energy, motivation, inspiration.

But the time to set goals is much earlier in those decades of life. While it's never too late, it's never too early. Don't waste time or your life. Do it yesterday. Or certainly today. Tomorrow might not come.

ABOUT THE AUTHORS

Richard "Digger" Phelps is an ESPN college basketball analyst. Before joining ESPN, he was one of America's most visible and successful college basketball coaches. The nickname "Digger" derives from his birthplace of Beacon, New York, where his father owned a funeral service.

He began his coaching career in 1963 as a graduate assistant at Rider College, where he had played basketball. After a move to the high school ranks, he got his first full assistant job in 1966 at the University of Pennsylvania. His first head coaching job came in 1970 at Fordham University. After leading the Rams to a 26–3 record in the 1970-71 season, he was named head coach at the University of Notre Dame.

During his 20 seasons at Notre Dame (1971–1991), his teams went 393–197, with 14 seasons of 20 wins or more. In 1978, Notre Dame made its only (men's) Final Four appearance to date. However, his most-remembered game was on January 19, 1974, when the Fighting Irish scored the last 12 points of the game to defeat top-ranked UCLA 71–70, ending the Bruins' record 88-game winning streak.

After leaving coaching, he headed Operation Weed and Seed for President George H. W. Bush, and also served as an observer in the 1993 elections in Cambodia. His broadcasting career began in 1993, with color commentary on the NCAA tournament for CBS. He joined ESPN the next season.

Jack Colwell is a political columnist for the *South Bend* (Indiana) *Tribune* and teaches journalism at the University of Notre Dame.